D0378647

A QUESTION
OF CHARACTER

A QUESTION OF CHARACTER

Life Lessons to Learn from Military History

THAD A. GAEBELEIN
RON P. SIMMONS

RED BRICK PRESS
New York

Red Brick Press
An Independent Imprint of Hatherleigh Press

Red Brick Press
An Independent Imprint of Hatherleigh Press
An Affiliate of W.W. Norton & Company, Inc.
5-22 46th Avenue, Suite 200
Long Island City, NY 11101
1-800-367-2550

Printed in Canada
This edition is printed on acid-free paper that meets the American
National Standards Institute z39-48 Standard.

Library of Congress Cataloging-in-Publication Data
Gaebelain, Thad A., 1956–
A question of character : life lessons to learn from military history /
Thad A. Gaebelein. Ron P. Simmons.
p. cm.
ISBN 1–57826–019–1 (alk. paper)
1. Character. 2. Leadership--Psychological aspects.
3. Psychology, Military--Case studies. I. Simmons,
Ron P., 1957–   II. Title.
BF818.G29 1998
170'.44--dc21   98–39862
                                                    CIP

All Red Brick Press titles are available for bulk purchase,
special promotions, and premiums. For more information,
please contact the manager of our Special Sales Department
at 1-800-367-2550.

Designed by DCDesign

10 9 8 7 6 5 4 3 2 1

CONTENTS

Part II: THE PROOF

DEDICATION

RON P. SIMMONS

To Diane, Lyndsey, Lauren and Leyla, I continually thank God for you!

Many thanks to the Simmons family across the country. Your constant support and encouragement never fails.

Henri & Mike Bertuch, your continual thirst for value and improvement have been an awesome example, both remarkable and invaluable.

THAD A. GAEBELEIN

To Elektra, Erika, Natalie and Andrew for your love and support.

To my father, who is my hero. To Colonel Doughty and Colonel Johnson for giving me the opportunity to teach and grow at such a tremendous institution.

Finally, to my father-in-law, Dr. X. Damianos, who, like my father, has demonstrated over the years the best of much of this book in his own life.

A FOREWORD
FROM RON SIMMONS

"Value behind the Value"

> *"... Above all a leader must be genuine...his own true self, not an imitation of some other, be that other ever so successful."*
>
> \- LINCOLN ANDREWS

IN 1993, I co-authored a technical business book, *Value-Directed Management*, oriented towards leaders in manufacturing and service-oriented businesses. The book offered the best of my own experiences in business and suggested the most effective leadership strategies to capture "added value." In my subsequent travels around the country and world, promoting my book, I have talked with countless business leaders about the correct measures of success for any organization. An interesting phenomenon emerged. Inevitably, every conversation about leadership began with competencies and competitive advantages, but somehow ended with thoughtful discussion about a person's character and integrity. It seemed that you could run the most profitable corporation in the world and still not be a good leader, still not insure continued success for the future. Those companies that possessed the greatest staying power, the lowest turnover rates and hardest working employees possessed something more intangible as well.

It began to dawn on me that there is something behind the competencies and innovative leadership strategies that contributes to a successful business. Something more basic struck a cord in the hearts of people I talked to when they contemplated the subject of leadership. That "something" is character.

Later I met Thad Gaebelein. When we discussed my new realizations on value-conscious leadership, he instantly regaled me with fascinating stories of military innovators, centuries past, who had successfully applied the same techniques. I have to admit that I was both crushed and delighted. Crushed with the realization that I was not original. I had been beaten to the punch by a few hundred years! Delighted, in knowing the themes I was developing were validated by "great captains" of war. Thad and I also came to the conclusion that there is more behind the value of any strategy or list of leadership competencies. This value behind the value is character, and this book is about the connection between successful leadership and the impact of the human element of character.

This book is for anyone, and its lessons can be applied as equally to business and military planning as they can to family and personal relationships. We all strive to be leaders in some sense, and we all want to be the best leaders we can. There's more to leadership than making critical decisions at the most opportune times — just like there's more to winning a battle than having the largest army.

Intrigued? We hope so. Read on.

Part I

THE PRINCIPLES

1 CHARACTER AND CHOICES

"Even at one third right, an honest leader—one who squarely faces mistakes, including his own—will take a company father than some fancy pants M.B.A. without character."

—INDUSTRY WEEK, MAY 1999

"Leadership is inherently neither good nor evil. It can serve either end. Leaders of character use their abilities to serve the public good, as best they can discern it."

—COL. LARRY DONNITHORNE (RET.)

WHY IS IT that the good guys always win? We've known the formula since the inception of Hollywood: the hero is tempted by the easy choice, the quick fix. Only by making the difficult choice — the right choice — will he prevail. And inevitably, he does make that choice, and remains the hero. Somehow, the villains never have such strength of character.

In business, there are heroes and villains as well, though the lines are never as clear cut as in the movies. What does it take to lead your business, your department, or your project through tough times? Why do some organizations exist behind obstructive walls while others build walls for support and strength? How wrong could you be and still have your employees follow you? These are the questions we pondered as we began to think about this book.

We've often heard that business is war, and there's some truth to that. Yet we prefer to qualify that statement. A business, like a military campaign, can only be successful if the troops are led by and contain people of character. Character, like munitions or supplies, is a must-have. It's what separates the lasting from the flash in the pan. Character — or lack of it — can destroy the mightiest of armies, as we will see.

Everywhere around us we see the negative by-products of failed character and corrupted leadership. Rising divorce rates, broken families, shameless greed in business, and cynical hypocrisy and immoral behavior among our leaders deeply concern us. In recent years, the alleged sexual indiscretions by leaders in our churches, our businesses — even in the presidency — show how the issue of character has exploded onto our national consciousness. Reams of material have been written on the topic of leadership and character.

This book is different from the traditional checklist methodology. There is a connection between character and leadership that reaches beyond the altruistic. We do not merely argue for good character on the basis of "being good for goodness sake." We believe that good character is the essential component for leaders in any competitive environment. Good character drives personal and professional conduct, not just our own, but others around us as well. In both the personal example a leader sets to his or her professional performance, good character is a crucial determinant for success.

The five federal service academies (Army, Navy, Air Force, Coast Guard, and Merchant Marine) are our nation's foremost leadership training institutions. Significantly, each academy begins with character building as the foundation for developing leaders for tomorrow. Each features the words character, integrity, and service prominently in their mission statements. Equally significant, almost all of the nation's top business schools are scrambling to add ethics courses to their curriculums. Obviously there is much more to leadership and management than being smart, talented, and well educated.

History provides us with great moments of contemplation with the benefit and clarity of hindsight. History, and particularly military history, has its clear winners and losers, its conquerors and its conquered, its rich and its poor, its successes and its failures. This book will tell the stories of men and women from military history who possessed a measure of character that set them apart from their opponents and contemporaries. They are of particular interest to us because their leadership was rooted in character and because we believe that their lessons can be applied to today's business or even home environment. We present examples from military history because in no other profession are the consequences for failure so extreme.

These leaders sought out opportunities rather than complain about obstacles. They consciously chose to "change the unit of measure," especially in the way they "measured" and treated people. This allowed them to unlock the tremendous potential in the human resources lying dormant within their organizations. What they succeeded in building and achieving was not the result of any superior technological advantage, or overwhelming manpower or material. In fact, in many cases their opponents outnumbered them and had "more, better stuff."

What they were able to do is take all of the same basic ingredients (available manpower, equivalent technology, and money), common to all their opponents, yet come up with a dramatically better product (army, doctrine, and strategy) than their rivals. How did they do it? What guiding principles did they use that are applicable to you and your enterprise? To find the answer to these questions, you must first decide for yourself how to answer history's deepest challenge to you: to lead or to follow.

The issue of character knows no boundaries. In every situation, in every time period, we have been confronted with issues of character. And one thing remains true: *Character is a Choice*.

Character is a Choice

Character won't find you-you have to want it!

There is a tremendous irony to the practice of aerial combat. Less than 5% of fighter pilots perform 80% of the kills. Accounting for this "Ace Factor" has been endlessly scrutinized and debated by military historians, scientists and strategists. One thing is certain. When any ace climbed into his aircraft, he did not strap into it, *he strapped it onto him.* He was going to make that plane do whatever it took to make a difference. To him, the vast majority of combat pilots were "quackin in the back" (merely following) or potential targets for the enemy.

The ace factor was a chosen attitude, an unquenchable thirst to improve. *It embodies the pursuit of excellence both professionally and personally.* Regardless of the kind of organization you work in, whether it is a business, non-profit charitable organization, school, community service, or church, are you merely "quackin in the back," just managing to survive, rather than thrive?

2 CHARACTER MEANS COMMITMENT

IN 1989, a powerful and venerable Wall Street firm collapsed. Forbes magazine wrote a penetrating article entitled "The Captains Who Didn't Go Down With The Ship" outlining the disaster. Essentially, through ill-conceived financial overreach, negligence, and sheer greed, the executive leadership of Thompson and McKinnon caused the firm's collapse. By itself, this business failure was not morally bad. Leaders often make mistakes, and Wall Street is notorious for spectacular financial failures. What was morally unconscionable was how the firm's top leadership had systematically pillaged the firm's assets, including their employee's pension fund, to feather their own nests, arranging bailouts with "golden parachutes." Of course, reasonable settlements and severance are an accepted practice. Yet what these executives arranged for themselves was outrageous.

These executives engineered their own escape

without a thought about those to whom they were responsible: the employees. Not only had the leadership inadvertently caused the demise of the company, they had escaped with the goods. In a sense they had robbed the very store they were supposed to be guarding.

A lack of accountability among leaders is dangerous and inexcusable. Worse, as in the case of Thompson and McKinnon, it will inevitably lead to the failure of any enterprise. Though it is possible for opportunistic leaders to shamelessly exploit certain "windows of opportunity" for their own self-aggrandizement, this outlook takes us into a jungle of mistrust, back-stabbing and chaos.

The conquests of any leader can be great or small, but to succeed, they must be planters — not pillagers. Planters sow seeds of integrity, trust, and competence in their fields. Pillagers steal and destroy seeking only to further their own goals. One seeks to build up. The other tears down. Planters work to cultivate long-term stability and security. Pillagers think only of today. They are perfectly willing to destroy future possibilities for the whole to benefit themselves.

In the wake of the 1980s savings and loan bank scandals, we witnessed a pervasive moral collapse of a number of white-collar professionals, who like the executives at Thompson and Mckinnon looted the very banks they were heading. They abused their trust. Men such as Michael Milkin and Ivan Boesky became the new icons of American business as they characterized and dominated the culture symbolized by the "predator's ball." While romantic at the time, this culture was superficial, treacherous, and constantly shifting. It was a house built upon sand. A house destined to collapse with the first fierce storm. Once the wheels of justice began to turn, Milkin and Boesky's windows of opportunity quickly materialized into prison windows.

Poor performance and mistakes on a leader's part are one thing — no one would ever expect a leader to always be right. Pillaging is another. Performance can be improved. Moral failings are much harder to fix. Moral failings undermine the employee's confidence in the level playing field of fairness, consistency, and due diligence within an organization. People simply will not fully invest themselves in an organization they feel is inherently unfair or suspicious — be it a business or relationship. The insidious by-products of malaise, mediocrity, and distrust begin to infect the corporate culture. People cower with timidity rather than demonstrate initiative. They spend more time watching their back instead of producing for the company. Involvement and interdependencies break down. The organization is merely going through the motions, where the workers become reluctant slaves rather than willing servants. Not surprisingly, the organization quickly loses its competitive edge. On this, the record of history is clear.

Sadly, however, "take no Prisoners," "go for the jugular," "show no mercy," and "slash and burn" remain popular slogans in our modern lexicon. They reflect the ruthless "go for broke" cultural and professional attitude of pillaging. This is an attitude that promotes the notion that nice guys finish last in today's competitive world. A notion that integrity and altruism are, for all practical purposes, antithetical to being competitive and successful in today's market-driven consumer culture. We reject these notions.

Whether in business, the military, politics, or even the clergy, leaders have basic choices to make that will profoundly affect their conduct. Whatever their sphere of influence, a leader must decide whether he will be a caretaker or a builder of the enterprise. The leader must also reconcile his or her position to competing notions of service. As leaders, are they there to serve the enterprise or is it there to serve them? In other words, are you there to make a difference? It is the quality of character in a leader that defines his or her decisions regarding these fundamental choices. Character drives notions of accountability, stewardship, personal conduct, use of people and resources, and measurements of success.

To choose to be a caretaker, interested in merely maintaining a status quo, is to ultimately doom your enterprise to failure in the long term: just as to choose to pillage will doom your enterprise to failure in the short term. We live in a competitive world that is constantly progressing. History is replete with examples of armies, businesses, and governments that were destined for defeat because their leaders refused to adapt and improve. It is not enough to be a planter — just to make the commitment to the organization. A good leader must also commit to grow the enterprise, to try new things, to adapt as the environment adapts.

For those who choose to make the commitment, Shakespeare's quote "ambition, the soldier's virtue" is only half-right. What prevents ambition from becoming obsession? What prevents a planter from becoming a pillager? Good character helps to harness ambition in a positive way. It enables leaders to be unselfish and see themselves as servants to the organization. Servant leaders are motivated by what is best for the organization; not necessarily what is best for themselves personally. As a result they will be far more open-minded to others' ideas of how to change and grow the business.

CHARACTER'S FIRST DEMAND

Character means commitment—and a conscious choice for growth

A leader with character will always think first of the organization he serves, not how the organization can serve him. A leader of character always has an eye on the future regarding the organization to which he has committed.

3 CHARACTER ALWAYS CATCHES UP

"The final estimate of men shows that history cares not one iota for the rank or title a man has borne or the office he has held, but only for the quality of his deeds and the character of his mind and heart."

— SAMUEL BRENGLE

TODAY THE character issue refuses to go away. In fact the debate has intensified. In 1998-1999, the character issue engulfed the highest office in the land, when President Clinton's presidency teetered on the brink because of a sex scandal involving a young White House intern. Bill Clinton is certainly not the first American President to be involved in sexual indiscretions. The difference for Bill Clinton is that these are not traditional times. In the past reporters overlooked the philandering of presidents, exercising restraint and discretion, refusing to cater to the prurient instincts of the public. In contrast,

Clinton, as well as other high profile leaders, must today endure the "no holds barred" glare of media scrutiny that Americans have come to rely on and demand.

Though a leader might have a right to govern as he or she chooses, serious character flaws certainly impinge on that ability. No one can argue that the recent impeachment hearings were not a huge national distraction from the business of the U.S. government. Good leadership, especially in this country, depends heavily on the consent of the governed. The issue here is trust. Once a leader breaches trust, confidence among those he leads erodes. Though some misdeeds like sexual indiscretions are not technically illegal, they are certainly ill advised and will invariably impinge on one's ability to lead.

Character flaws not only impinge on your ability to lead, but also dictate your legacy. President Richard Nixon is remembered for lying and Watergate, not for the spectacular foreign policy success of opening China. Benedict Arnold is synonymous with betrayal and renowned as a traitor. Overshadowed was his bravery, sacrifice and brilliance at Bemis Heights which carried the Americans to victory at the Battle of Saratoga in 1777, which was arguably the most decisive battle ever fought in the western hemisphere. There is no doubt that Clinton's effectiveness as a leader and role model has been severely tarnished as a result of the impeachment hearings. While Americans have and may continue to support Clinton, the longer-term effects of this American ordeal have yet to be seen. Certainly the reputation and respect traditionally afforded the position of President of the United States has to be greatly repaired.

Yet you do not have to be President of the United States to be under the glare of scrutiny as a leader today. Times are changing. Leaders in all areas — political, religious, corporate, educational and community based — face greater scrutiny and accountability than ever before. Increasing awareness and laws regarding sexual harassment and discrimination are now a given in the workplace. The same with equal opportunity in hiring. Your personal conduct does matter and a growing plethora of governmental regulations seeks to insure that.

CHARACTER'S LEGACY

Character always catches up

Character issues are not lightly ignored. From the highest position of authority to the head of a household, character matters, even if it doesn't appear to initially.

4 CHARACTER CREATES PASSION

"Wars may be fought with weapons but they are won by men. It is the spirit of the men who follow and the man who leads that gains the victory."

—GEORGE PATTON

AMERICAN GENERAL George Patton said it best. "It is not the sharpness of the bayonet, but rather the gleam in the eye of the person wielding it that will break the enemy line." In an age when we are all so easily seduced by marketing gimmicks and the glamour of technology, Patton reminds us that it is still the human element that is decisive. And the human element is best swayed and infused with passion by good character. It is character that puts the "gleam in the eye" of a leader as well as the subordinates. A leader with character can create the passion necessary to separate a status quo organization from a truly successful and growing organization.

The ultimate resource of any organization is not necessarily its product, technology, or property, but rather its people. Organizations that rely too heavily on externally imposed discipline will experience a diminishing competitive edge. When discipline is externally imposed, leaders expend much of their time and energy making unmotivated subordinates accomplish the routine. Less time or energy is available for innovation and improvement. Management spends more time making sure people are doing things correctly than asking if the things they are doing are correct.

The future belongs to leaders of organizations that can harness the true passion of its leaders into the development of internally motivated self-discipline among its employees. In a sense it is the choice between creating a workplace where people want to work or where they have to work. Modern business leaders search for "added value" and synergy to break away from the competition. Just being incrementally more efficient is now no longer enough. Something more is needed. That something more is character — and character creates passion.

Swedish King Gustavus Adolphus, with a pitifully small strategic base, became a "major player" during the Thirty Year's War in 1631. Napoleon Bonaparte's Grande Armeè would convert the social chaos of a revolution into tremendous flexibility and superiority on battlefields. In contrast "caretaker" minded European monarchs kept their heads in the sand and got clobbered for more than a decade. In our own century, Air Chief Marshall Hugh Dowding, head of Britain's Fighter Command in World War II, would leverage a ridiculously small force into staving off an overwhelmingly superior Nazi juggernaut. Senior General Nguyen Thi Dinh rose from utter poverty to become the deputy commander of all the Viet Cong forces fighting in South Vietnam. Her efforts were crucial in mobilizing her people to defeat an American superpower.

The successes created by these men and women were far superior to the competition. Ironically, their superiority was not based on technology or strength in numbers. The common denominator was their character as leaders, which enabled them to implement radical organizational and doctrinal changes. These changes lead to synergistic leaps in effectiveness and productivity. More specifically, their new organizations far better motivated and utilized people, which in the end carried the day on battlefields.

A leader of good character is unselfish, humble, honest, and secure within himself. His self-esteem is not based on the accolades, privilege or power of his position, but rather in the confidence he has in his ability to lead successfully. Such a humble leader is more apt to enfranchise others and share credit and power. He is not threatened by a subordinate's talent or success, but rather seeks to advance his subordinates. He is interested in involving the best of people, not taking advantage of them.

To share, to give, to be open-minded, and to trust others is easier said than done. To do so a leader must be secure enough within himself to willingly be vulnerable. As humans it is natural for us to crave prestige and power. We share or shed power with great reluctance. While the empowerment of those below is lauded in management and business journals today, many leaders find that this is much easier advised than put into practice. To give up power in order to invest that power in a subordinate definitely entails risk. Subordinates, after all, can and do fail. Worse, their failure can have drastic consequences for you. Consequently, this vulnerability of a leader must balance with realism. "Powering down" authority and decision making must be to subordinates of proven competence. Nevertheless, any leader who seeks to empower subordinates must always be willing to accept a degree of personal vulnerability and risk. But the rewards can be huge.

Gustavus Adolphus, Napoleon, Dowding and Nguyen Thi Dinh were great sythnesizers of the best of other people's ideas and abilities. But the world is full of good ideas. Yet their genius far exceeded merely understanding and integrating the ideas of others. What made these leaders unique was their character, which enabled them to turn these ideas into reality. They could not have done so without the buy-in of the people in their organizations, and the confidence in their ability to try untested ideas. They were quick to share credit and well-placed power with others. Because of their character, they were secure enough in themselves to go against rigid societal norms and implement the untested ideas. They challenged the accepted assumptions and traditions of their time. They tore down traditional walls that stifled initiative and curtailed flexibility. In doing so they created radical new organizational structures that shared authority, power and rewards. Their egos were not threatened by opening up the franchise.

They knew that the success of their organization rode on the initiative and performance of all those in their organizations — not just the superhuman efforts of the boss. Their organizations were successful because, from top to bottom, their personnel were inspired and empowered. When they flung their armies into the chaos of battle, they had confidence that all the thousands under their command would carry the day. They knew that their subordinates and soldiers would more often make better decisions and conduct more successful actions than the opposing force because they had that "gleam in the eye" and operated in a structure that encouraged it. When your business enterprise is flung into the chaos of a competitive marketplace, do those under you have that "gleam in the eye?"

CHARACTER'S EFFECT

Character creates passion

A leader with character knows that the people in the organization are its greatest asset. Their confidence in and passion for a leader will allow the leader to distribute responsibility throughout the organization.

It takes character to empower.

It takes empowerment to succeed.

5 CHARACTER: THE FOUR - PART COMBINATION

IF EXCELLENCE, total quality, competitiveness, global strategy, and empowerment have been among the most popular buzzwords of the nineties, what are the most likely buzzwords of the next century? We don't care. What we do care about is teaching an approach to achieving effective relationships and lasting value in your endeavors. We've already reviewed some of what character means — commitment, a chance to do good, an opportunity to create passion. In this chapter we'll introduce our four-part definition of character — we call them the "ins." Without them, you'll soon be "out" as an effective leader. Development of these character values provides the essential backbone for success. These values are the foundational elements that brought victory to battlefields and can bring a new vitality to your personal leadership. We hope you will use these four values as an internal strategy to affect your life in practical ways.

Involvement: Make those in your organization actively interested in pursuing value.

Interdependence: Create teamwork and teams within your organization that you can rely on—and that can rely on each other.

Ingraining: Your organization must take character values as the norm.

Indicators: You need the right set of indicators to tell the score.

These four values are essential in order to provide increased value, because each one addresses how an individual, organization or even armies deal with its internal management, material, informational and human resources. Even though each one is different, they are mutually reinforcing, and each is critical to success. They are the four-number combination to a safe. In the absence of even one number, the valuables are beyond reach.

6 CHARACTER VALUE #1: INVOLVEMENT

A Tale of Two Battles

It was early in the morning when the courier awakened General George Gordon Meade in his tent. The courier's face was grim. The news, the general thought to himself, must be bad, perhaps a death in the family. Yet the message was altogether unexpected. It was urgent from President Lincoln. General Meade had just been appointed commander of the Union Army of the Potomac.

Normally, being appointed commander of an army is the crowning achievement to any officer's career. But these were not ordinary times and this was not an ordinary army. The country was in the middle of a civil war that was proving to be bloodier and more horrible than anyone could have imagined. The Confederacy was putting up a tremendous fight. The Union army had been repeatedly thrashed. The list of defeats was long and sobering: Bull Run, The Peninsula Campaign, Second Bull Run, Chancellorsville, and Fredericksburg were all painful reminders of missed opportunities and failure. The inescapable fact was that the Union army had been out-maneuvered, out-generaled, and out-fought by the Confederates. Meade's appointment marked the fifth change of command for The Union Army of the Potomac in only two years. Morale was at an all-time low. Command of this Army was a job for which few people were qualified and even fewer people wanted. Meade's staff and other senior officers must have looked at him as if he were the unluckiest man in the world.

The timing could not have been worse for the new commander. Without any chance at all to settle into command he had to act. The date was June 28, 1863 and General Lee's Army of Northern Virginia was on the move again, headed north. Scouting reports were astonishing, with reports of Confederate forces spread out across southern Pennsylvania. What was Lee's objective? Harrisburg, Washington, or Philadelphia. One thing was certain: Meade had to protect the city of Washington. The only way he could do that was to stay between the capitol and Lee's Army. If he failed or lost to Lee on northern soil, Lee could take Washington and end the war.

It began to dawn on Meade that the North could actually lose this war. The stakes could not have been higher. Ordering the only option he had, Meade commanded the army to march northwest to intercept Lee at a small town that was in the center of where scouts had spotted Lee's army. Meade did not know it at the time, but he had just made an absolutely vital decision in which he could influence the action. The name of the small town was Gettysburg.

When Colonel Gouverneur K. Warren of the union army awoke that morning of July 3, 1863 he took stock of his situation. It was going to be another blistering hot summer day. The battle at Gettysburg was not going well. The day before had seen the Union line north of the town broken. The Confederates now occupied the town. The Union forces had retreated to high ground just south of town to make a stand. He knew that today would be decisive as the full strength of both armies arrived. How ironic, he thought, that in this battle the South was attacking from the north and the North was defending from the south.

Warren was a senior Engineer Officer located by a Federal signaling station placed at the southernmost tip of the Union line. This was a location selected for its good observation and apparent safety from the battle. The benign hilltop, referred to by the locals as Little Round Top, seemed far enough away from the action yet offered a great view of the entire Union position.

Warren, like everyone else, knew that the war

was reaching a climax. And he was worried. He knew Meade well and was glad he was in charge. Meade had a solid reputation as a tough fighter and a man of integrity. He believed that Meade would be better than the previous leaders but would still need all the help he could get. There had been too many defeats and the Confederate Army was too far North. This was a battle the North could not lose.

Late in the afternoon, Warren lifted his long scope and surveyed the Union line. It was like a giant fishhook, running north up Cemetery Ridge, then hooking east around Cemetery and Culp's hills. Then he scanned out front. What he saw shocked him. Confederate forces were marshalling in the southern part of the area. They were on their way to attack through his territory, and there were no significant Union infantry forces down here to defend the Union left flank. Warren knew that if Confederates ever took Little Round Top, their artillery could then be repositioned there to rake the Union line with devastating enfilading fire (fire directed along the length of a position). In addition, from there succeeding Confederate attacks could easily envelope and compromise the whole Union position. Disaster loomed and he knew it.

Warren correctly surmised that the signal unit of a dozen or so men waving flags was not going to stop a Confederate assault. He knew he had to get infantry up there very quickly. But how to do that? Regular channels would take much too long just to

get the word to Meade at Headquarters. Acting on
his own initiative, Warren frantically intercepted a
reserve infantry unit just converging on Gettysburg,
urgently requesting them to override their standing
orders and divert immediately to Little Round Top.
It worked. At the other end of this frantic request
was Colonel Joshua Chamberlin, Commanding
Officer of the 20th Maine Regiment, who "double
timed" his regiment up the backside of Little Round
Top to get in position. Arriving not a moment too
soon, Chamberlin deployed his unit only minutes
before the first Confederate attacks hit.

Chamberlin, a former Bowdin College history
professor, successfully led his men that day in
what was arguably the most important small unit
tactical action of the entire Civil War. Vastly outnumbered, his regiment withstood three successive furious Confederate assaults. Because of the
densely wooded terrain, the rebels were able to
more easily draw close to the defensive line. The
fighting became hand to hand. Exhausted and out
of ammunition, it seemed as if one more confederate thrust would break the Union position.
Chamberlin knew he could not absorb one more
determined assault. To remain on the defense was
sure defeat. In desperation Chamberlin got cre-
ative. He ordered his men to fix bayonets and
counterattacked back down the hill, catching the
regrouping Confederate infantry completely by

surprise. They bolted. Joshua Chamberlin had held the Union left flank on the second day.

The Union Army of the Potomac would go on to win the battle on the third day in dramatic fashion by slaughtering Confederate Divisional General Picket's ill-conceived charge into the strength of the Union center. Meade's second crucial decision was to stand and fight that third day. But that decision wouldn't have been possible if it were not for Warren and Chamberlin's second day heroics.

Only two months later, on another faraway front in rural northern Georgia, General Rosecrans' Union Army of the Cumberland was relentlessly pressing on to Atlanta to bisect the South. Squaring off at a place the local Indians had named Chickamuaga, or river of death, Confederate General Bragg finally decided to give battle and check Rosecrans' advance. The stakes were high. Though Gettysburg had been a costly failure, it was a failure on northern soil. Failure to halt Rosecrans would threaten Atlanta, a vital Confederate infrastructure point and state capitol.

After some early sparring, both sides drew up parallel to each other on the morning of September 20, 1863. While inspecting his line earlier that morning, Rosecrans roundly yelled at and publicly humiliated one of his division commanders. Roscran's mistake — brutal admonishing of a subordinate in public — would prove to be costly. Such public corrective action can rob the recipient of his dignity and engender a deep-seated hatred or intimidation towards his superior, or even, the entire organization.

Later that day, Rosecrans ordered this particular commander to leave the line for another assignment. Standard operating procedure dictated that you should never vacate your place in the line until your relief has arrived, so an inadvertent gap in your own line would not be created. Yet this is what happened. This division commander was determined to follow his new orders to the letter, for fear of risking another browbeating from Rosecrans. As fate would have it, his unit's withdrawal before relief arrived left a yawning gap in the Union line, the exact spot where the Confederate main attack landed.

Needless to say, the Confederates broke through. Rosecrans lost his nerve. The Union army was routed and beat a hasty retreat all the way back to Chattanooga. In the words of President Lincoln, Rosecrans was "confused and stunned, like a duck hit on the head." Even worse for the Union, plans to bisect the south were set back, giving the South a needed victory and some invaluable breathing space.

What Lessons Were Learned?

In both battles it was subordinates, not their superiors, that instigated the decisive action. In today's world as well, success or failure of any organization often rides on the performance and quick thinking of its subordinates. Gettysburg was a battle won not by Meade's brilliant Generalship, but rather by the sum total of numerous actions and initiatives taken by men like Warren and Chamberlin. When confronted by the need to make decisions independent of their commander, they felt free to exercise their initiative. This was especially valuable in the ever-changing circumstances of Gettysburg. Put simply, Meade had a positive command environment. Contrast this environment with the one created by Rosecrans, in which a key subordinate knowingly ignored a basic and vital proceedure because he was intimidated. Because of this negative command environment, Rosecrans had robbed his army of its most valuable natural asset: the confidence and intelligence of its personnel.

Involvement is the process by which employees voluntarily and actively pursue increments to value. If any organization is to succeed in today's highly competitive environment, employees must be involved creatively. An organization is at a severe disadvantage if its employees are merely automatons carrying out orders. In order for additional values like interdependence and integration to have their desired effects on increasing values, the employees must be convinced of the need for them and be involved in their implementation.

At Gettysburg and Chickamauga we witnessed contrasting episodes of involvement. Involving people of proven competence in a positive manner is vital because the boss simply can't be everywhere at once. A good leader must learn to create positions below him that are filled with employees he trusts, and who trust him. Like it or not, a commitment to positive involvement is a must and it begins with respect for others and their personal dignity. Loyalty is a two-way street. If you expect it from your subordinates, then you must demonstrate it to them. Whether a leader realizes it or not, subordinates play a crucial role, one that can easily determine success or failure. If success is your goal, then positive involvement is a must, unless of course you desire to be a smacked duck.

Character Value #1

Involvement

Make those in your organization actively interested in pursuing value. They are vital to your success — make sure they know it. Create an environment where innovation is applauded, crisis are met head-on, and decisive action is rewarded.

7 CHARACTER VALUE #2: INTERDEPENDENCE

Interdependence and Isandhlawana

Kings are not the only ones who crave to build their own empires. We all do. No matter how large or small our individual responsibilities are, we all instinctively protect what we think is ours. "Turf wars" and "protecting one's turf" are all too common expressions in any profession. Sometimes it seems that the smaller our slice of the pie, the more we fight over it. For example, when asked why the back-stabbing and infighting is so pronounced amongst university professors within academic departments, Henry Kissinger (who had served on the Harvard faculty) unflinchingly responded, "because the stakes are so low." But in the right set of circumstances, empire building — even on a small scale — can produce consequences more severe than anyone would expect.

In January, 1879, the arrogant Lord Chelmsford led a modern British expeditionary force into the hinterland of Natal, South Africa. He was determined to teach the restless Zulu natives a lesson in British supremacy. Armed with the latest Martini-Henry rifles, his soldiers could each fire six aimed shots a minute out to 600 yards. In coordinated firing ranks, the deadly wall of steel disciplined British regulars could throw out was awesome. Zulu infantry, on the other hand, were hopelessly outclassed. Though long on courage and physical endurance, Zulu warriors were armed only with spears and canvas shields. Despite their enormous numerical advantage of 40,000 to 3000, the Zulu army seemed destined to serve as target practice for the British. Only a miracle, or a major British mistake, could rescue the Zulu army from slaughter. The British obliged.

Lord Chelmsford split his force, leaving half at Isandhlwana, while he took off with the rest in search of Zulus and glory. By such action Chelmsford took a huge risk. Violating a key principle of war, mass, Chelmsford divided his force without having any real information about the true disposition of the enemy. Worse, he left vague and unclear orders to two remaining key subordinate commanders regarding chain of command and objective.

When the battle began at Isandhlwana, British soldiers were amazed at the sheer numbers of swarming Zulus. Nevertheless they went about their grim task of firing into the waves of approaching humanity. Their volley fire cut like steel scythes through the Zulu formations. Unfortunately, the bickering subordinate commanders never agreed on a single unified defensive plan or on who would assume overall command. This breakdown of British leadership violated the two utmost principles of war: Unity of Command and Objective. Consequently, the British defense became disjointed and vulnerable. Much of the available British manpower was employed at cross-purposes. Simple actions that should have been taken automatically, such as circling and turning over wagons, were not taken.

To make matters worse, high rates of volley fire meant a very high consumption of bullets. In a short time, many British soldiers on the firing lines had used up their standard issue of ammunition. They clamored for rapid resupply. A crisis was emerging. If the British could not maintain their rates of fire, they risked being swamped by an overwhelming Zulu onslaught. It was here that the British supply system broke down.

Normal supply and ammunition distribution is considered pedestrian, involving mostly paperwork and accountability procedures. It is ruled by a rare breed known in all armies as the supply Sergeant. In the "empire" of supply, supply Sergeants rule absolutely. Anyone who has ever served in the army quickly learns rule number one: never cross the supply sergeant. From beans to bullets, he's got the stuff you need to be a hero. He can make it easy or stonewall you with procedure.

On this day, the chief British supply Sergeant was an officious bureaucrat more interested in enforcing his procedures than in alleviating the darkening tactical circumstances. Soon a long line of anxious soldiers stood at his wagon, awaiting reissue. Above the din of battle, one could hear the slackening of British fire due to units running low on bullets. At this point, the supply Sergeant should have been heaving ammo boxes of the wagon as fast as he could. Instead he continued to rule his empire as he wished: dolling out ammunition in an excruciatingly slow and meticulous manner. Disaster loomed.

While the British fire slackened appreciably, the Zulus were able to rush across the killing ground in massive numbers and literally swamp the British soldiers. Armed with spears, in overwhelming numbers, the Zulus slaughtered the entire British force to a man. Chelmsford, who had been miles away with the other half of his army, returned later that evening to view a blood-soaked field of 1300 skewered British regulars. This humiliating defeat reverberated all the way to hallowed governmental chambers of Whitehall in London and shook the British government.

Every relationship, business or organization has an internal chain or linkage of successive activities. These can be as varied as receiving and communicating orders in a fast food restaurant, drilling and stamping in a machine shop, or product promotion and customer contact in a marketing department. For the British expeditionary force, it was the formulation and dissemination of battle plans as well as the requesting and receiving of ammunition. These are interdependencies.

Interdependence is the extent of the linkage between two successive activities or events. Irrespective of context, the tighter the linkage (the stronger the interdependence), the greater the value or efficiency. In other words, more teamwork and less individualism and "turfdom" will bring about success.

At Isandhlwana, because of the myopic perspective of a few single individuals, crucial interdependencies broke down. The otherwise highly efficient war machine of a modern British expeditionary force sputtered then collapsed. Of course single individuals do make a difference, but so do the strength or weakness of interdependencies within any organization. In the end, stronger interdependence is as much an attitude or mindset of unselfishness that facilitates teamwork as it is a flow chart or personnel-manning roster.

Character Value #2

Interdependence

Foster teamwork.

Create teams within your organization that you can rely on and that can rely on each other.

It's not just about involving people — it's about involving them in a structure where they have to rely on others as well as themselves.

It's about linking tasks correctly and efficiently with teams that understand the value of those links.

8 CHARACTER VALUE # 3: INDICATORS

"Garbage In Garbage Out"

How are we doing? What's the score? Is it cost effective? How do we improve? The right set of indicators will tell you the score!

During the summer of 1965 in the Ia Drang valley of Vietnam, a single U.S. battalion successfully fought off a much larger North Vietnamese Army (NVA) force and inflicted tremendous casualties on them. From this experience, we concluded that through our superior technology and firepower, we could win a war in Vietnam. "Search and destroy" and "find, fix, and finish" the enemy became our modus operendi. By using these methods, we would bleed the Communists white. Attrition thus became our strategy in Vietnam, the "body count" our primary indicator of success.

Unfortunately, like the strategy, the indicator was flawed. Body counts could easily be, and often were, inflated or misleading. Analysis based on objective data is only as good as the data itself. If the data is flawed your indicator will be flawed as well. Cynical American Army staff officers referred to this as "garbage in: garbage out." Nor did this objective indicator take into account the subjective nature of the will of the enemy. President Lyndon Johnson joked about how he would "raise Ho Chi Minh's leg one inch at a time" until Ho's pain threshold was reached and he quit the fight. What he didn't count on was that Ho was willing to have his leg ripped off if doing so would win the conflict. It's a safe bet that, if the indicators are false, then your entire strategy or plan could result in failure while you remain blissfully unaware.

Secretary of Defense Robert McNamara assured President Kennedy that, "Every quantitative measurement we have shows we're winning this war." Later General Westmoreland and President Johnson talked about "the light at the end of the tunnel." They believed that their strategy of attrition would ultimately bring the enemy to its knees and they had their statistics to back it up. In retrospect, it's easy to see why the Tet Offensive of January 1968 was such a shock to the American public. Seemingly out of nowhere, Communist forces were able to launch massive surprise attacks throughout all of South Vietnam. Hadn't we been told that victory was in sight?

The American public was stunned. If we had been beating the enemy so badly for so long, then how could they muster the strength to launch an all-out nation-wide offensive against us? This "weakened" enemy was even able to take over our own embassy in Saigon! The American public was confounded. Every armchair strategist sitting in front of his TV watching the nightly news and counting bodies (ours now) concluded that something was not right. What we had been told about imminent victory did not square with the bloody reality we saw on our TV sets. Even though our military commanders claimed that we had won a great victory by counterattacking and inflicting tremendous casualties on the enemy, General Westmoreland still asked for additional reinforcements of 250,000 men! Asking for another quarter of a million men, after telling us we were on the verge of victory, did not sound like a war that could be won anytime soon. The American public quite simply found the president and his generals hard to believe.

Trust had been broken. After Tet record numbers of Americans actively began protesting the war. President Johnson's credibility plummeted. Less than two months later, he went on national TV to tell the nation he would seek peace and would not run again for re-election. The Tet Offensive cost

Johnson his Presidency, but it was also a military watershed for the entire Vietnam conflict. After Tet, we would seek disengagement, rather than outright victory, and a gradual withdrawal would begin.

Indicators matter. They are the criteria by which an organization evaluates itself. Get them right and you have a much better chance of pursuing the correct course. Get them wrong, you have potential disaster. The trick is getting the correct balance of objective and subjective indicators. Even more important, in a personal sense, is learning to recognize indicators when you are operating outside an organizational value system. In a sense indicators are the guardian angels of other character values. They keep watch over our actions and achievements, counseling restraint or redoubled efforts where necessary. They serve as a mirror reflecting not only our level of performance but also the processes, behaviors, and assumptions that will be beneficial in the long run.

CHARACTER VALUE #3

Indicators

You need the right set of indicators to tell you the score. And you need to trust and follow those indicators, even if they're not what you want to hear.

9 CHARACTER VALUE # 4: INGRAINING

Romans vs. the Dustbins

Popular clichès such as "History is bunk" and the "dustbins of history" reflect the growing arrogance of our modern technological age. We are tempted to think we do not have much to learn from our past, especially the ancient past.

How would you like to be the CEO of an organization that has maintained world dominance for centuries? That kind of staying power yields such wealth, power, and influence that it is almost unimaginable. In a world that measures time in increasingly smaller and smaller increments, 80 years, indeed even eight years of dominance seems remarkable by today's standards. But 800 years! That is what the Romans achieved.

The Romans were renowned for many things: law, government, administration, architecture, infrastructure, and their army. Many components of these things heavily influence our society today. Roman tradition can be seen in our government, civil service, jurisprudence, and city planning.

But it was the Roman conduct of war that insured their world dominance. For eight centuries the Roman Army was unable to be defeated by any army in the world. Of course, as with any army, they lost some battles, but they always won the war. Eight centuries is a long time. How did this organization stay on top for so long?

For starters, military historians point out that the Romans saw war as a business. Their military system reflected a professional "soldier" approach to war, as opposed to the prevailing individualistic "warrior" cultures of the time. Soldiers work as a team towards common, pre-planned goals. Warriors tend to fight undisciplined and individualistically in pursuit of bloodsport and glory.

In taking a business-like approach to war, Romans maintained a remarkable objectivity in putting together combat organizations. Even more, they were consistently open to change and reform. Over the many years of their supremacy, the Romans continually adjusted and evolved the structure, leadership, and format of their fighting formations in facing new opponents and terrain. This was balanced with a remarkable perseverance. No one was more patient and successful at siege warfare as the

Romans. In short, they were professionals committed to excellence.

Part of a commitment to excellence is thinking a whole problem through and then being willing to pay the price for a realistic solution. Beginning in 117 AD, under Emperor Hadrian, the Romans consolidated their vast empire. The defense of the empire was a tremendous undertaking involving the protection of thousands of miles of frontiers against numerous enemies. The Roman solution was a clever blend of static and maneuver defensive techniques. They fortified where practicable and adjusted boundaries along natural defensive terrain features such as the Rhine and Danube rivers. This strategy required the costly construction of over 200 miles of fixed fortifications, of which Hadrian's Wall across the neck of northern England is the most noteworthy. They also built thousands of miles of roads so they could rapidly shuttle their soldiers to trouble spots when needed. This maximized their inherent advantage of interior lines. Thus, some legions could remain forward deployed. Some could be held in reserve but still be within mutually supporting distance. This was successful for centuries. They confronted the whole problem, created a comprehensive solution, and spent the money and resources to implement it.

Even more important than the overall strategy or the building of roads was the building of the

"Centurianate," the professional leadership core of the Roman army. Centurions were the equivalent of sergeants and officers — those who make an army function once the generals have given the orders. They were the backbone of the Roman Army, and were world-renowned for their unswerving discipline. A Roman Centurion was supported by a society and political system which supplied and paid him well. Centurions had the bravery of warriors yet often subordinated their individualism to the collective good of the army. They were committed to Rome and to winning. If that meant sacrifice, they were ready to die. If it meant reform, they were willing to change or adjust or re-train regardless of personal cost. Like most good leaders, they were men of integrity. In the New Testament, Jesus Christ Himself upholds a Centurion as a model of faith and integrity. The values that made Centurions so unique were values ingrained into all Centurions — values taken as givens.

Ingraining is the process by which people develop norms and beliefs within the organization. Certain ways of thinking and doing become taken for granted, even if they have not been explicitly stated. Ingraining is the quality that insures long-term success. As an institution, the Roman Army successfully ingrained several core values into its Centurionate: discipline, honor, excellence, subordination of self, bravery, sacrifice, careful planning, and a business-like approach to war. These core values were transmitted from generation to generation. Even today, the word "centurion" evokes a feeling of dedication and discipline. These ingrained values yielded centuries of dominance for the Roman Empire. In terms of longevity and success, the Romans stand unparalleled in human experience.

Maybe it's not so much bunk after all.

Character Value #4

Ingraining

Your organization must take character values as the norm.

You want loyalty? Exhibit loyalty. Expect it. Reward it.

The same for honor, teamwork, dedication and commitment to excellence.

To sum up:

Character Value #1...Involvement

Remember to demonstrate respect for others.
Don't make General Rosecran's mistake — or it will cost you.

Character Value #2...Interdependence

Promote: Teamwork and the development of principles that are designed to serve the needs of your organization.
Don't let your Supply Sergeants build empires.

Character Value #3...Indicators

Learn to recognize indications when you are operating outside your value system.
Don't rely on faulty data to make critical decisions.

Character Value #4...Ingraining

Constantly refine and reinforce your core values.
Remember the Romans and 800 years of dominance.

None of these values will work alone. We've already seen that unchecked involvement of employees can result in empire building. There's no use in trying to ingrain certain principles into the members of your organization if there's no method in place for different departments to work together.

Taken together, however, these values can add tremendous value to your organization. We've already discussed some examples from military history where these values have had an enormous effect. The second half of this book will offer extended examples of how these values work together.

Part II

THE
PROOF

10 FROM THE JAWS OF DEFEAT: GUSTAVUS

NO ONE could have guessed, or even possibly imagined, how the day was going to turn out, least of all the Swedish king. By noon of September 17, 1631, on that remote field at Breitenfeld, Germany, the day was turning into a disaster. That morning King Gustavus Adolphus watched helplessly as his best laid plans to defeat the Imperialist Catholic army of General Tilly went hopelessly astray.

As Gustavus scanned the battlefield, he could see that his right flank was under heavy and repeated cavalry assault, but seemed to be holding. This might have provided momentary relief, yet catastrophe now unexpectedly struck on his left flank. His 18,000-man allied Saxon force, representing over forty percent of his total combat power, literally ran away! His entire left flank was now utterly exposed. And to compound the Saxon betrayal, the fleeing soldiers managed to stop and loot the Swedish supply base on their way out.

Gustavus, who had begun the day with a numerical advantage, was now significantly outnumbered and staring at his own possible annihilation. To complicate matters, the fact that his rear supply area was in flames eliminated the possibility of an orderly withdrawal from the situation. His opponent, French General Johan Tzerclaes Tilly, held the high ground, with the prevailing winds blowing gunpowder smoke back toward the Swedish line. In short, the king's tactical position looked hopeless.

On the other side of the field, the 70-year old cagey General Tilly must have been relishing the opportunity to defeat the young upstart Swede. Tilly's generalship had always been traditional and conservative. All the years of waiting in this seemingly endless conflict, known as the Thirty Years War, had finally paid off. Tilly seized the moment to administer the coup de grace. He ordered his main infantry force to "incline to the right" and smash into the unguarded Swedish left and roll up Gustavus' line. What a glorious capstone to his long career, he must have thought.

What little the Swedish king could see through his stinging and smarting eyes was not good. In fact it was terrifying. Through the fog of war he glimpsed the awesome spectacle of fifteen massive tercios less than half a mile away marching downhill towards his weakened position. It must have been an awesome sight indeed. A tercio is a huge square formation densely packed with up to three thousand men, all carrying an assortment of eight to twelve foot long pikes and occasionally interspersed with Arquebusers, or musketmen. Tercios literally looked like a cross between a gigantic porcupine and a turtle. And fifteen of these fearsome formations, bristling with thousands of sharp pointy objects, were bearing down on him.

At any other time during the bloody Thirty Years War, this maneuver would have won the day for Tilly. But it was not to be. For despite all that was going wrong, the Swedish army under Gustavus was not your typical tercio-style army of the seventeenth century. In fact, Gustavus' army was radically different in terms of combat organization, make-up, and leadership. The Swedish army was composed of much smaller formations of "squadrons" and "brigades."

As Gustavus watched Tilly's tercios rumble forward, he realized now was when he would finally see what his new army could really accomplish. With characteristic boldness, he ordered 4000 men, under the subordinate command of Marshal Horn, to pivot his array of squadrons and brigades ninety degrees from the front and rush over to meet Tilly's oncoming onslaught of fifteen tercios in order to shore up the left flank. Simultaneously, Gustavus sent two more brigades sweeping around Horn's left to hit the tercios on their farthest right. With all his remaining forces, Gustavus administered his own coup de grace. He ordered another capable subordinate, Marshal Baner, to leave the center of battle, and wheel all the way around and behind the tercios' left flank. Every one of these maneuvers was considered virtually impossible at that time. But they did it. In short order, the rapid mobility of the Swedish formations had enabled the army to encircle Tilly's lumbering leviathan.

What followed was slaughter. The surrounding squadrons laid off about fifty yards away from each of the huge tercios and poured musket and cannon fire into them from every side. Whenever the tercios tried to lumber away, the smaller squadrons' superior mobility allowed them to keep the fifty yard standoff range constant, all the while continuing to pour deadly fire into the hapless tercios.

By nightfall Tilly's once proud army was dead, wounded or captured. Tilly himself was seriously wounded and left wondering what had happened to his sure victory. Just a short while before, Tilly had been on the verge of triumph. For over two hundred years tercios had dominated the battlefield. He had fought this battle by the book! Yet almost as quickly as a flash of lightning, his army had been surrounded and then annihilated by a new force that moved faster and hit harder than anything he had ever witnessed. Even more humiliating was that Gustavus' force had been smaller and had no apparent technological advantage. How did the Swede do it? How had he created such a force?

11 CHARACTER VALUES IN ACTION: GUSTAVUS

GUSTAVUS' ARMY highlighted the dramatic effect of synergy because he was able to put into action all four character values: involvement, interdependence, indicators and ingraining. Though outnumbered that day with no technological advantage, the Swedish army's effectiveness at Breitenfeld was made possible because Gustavus had created an organization whose value far exceeded the sum of its parts. In every way Gustavus could be thought of as a "value-directed manager." Let us return to that day in 1631 to see how the Swedish king spun the combination of the four character values to unlock his organization's potential and win.

Gustavus made important reforms within his army, most of which defied all the conventions of the time, and they paid off handsomely for him.

He organized his army into "squadrons" of approximately 400 men, half with muskets, half with pikes. As opposed to the huge tercio squares, the much smaller squadrons were slender, rectangular, more mobile, linear-shaped formations. Though smaller, the Swedish Squadrons actually allowed more musketmen to be efficiently employed on line in ranks in order to achieve higher rates of volley fire. In addition, incorporated into the Swedish infantry formations were much smaller, three-pound shot "regimental" cannons easily moved by one horse or three men. The purpose of Gustavus' squadrons was to maximize the growing effectiveness of gunpowder weapons with the ability of the pikemen to ward off cavalry or infantry charges. The agile squadrons could quickly combine together to form brigades for even greater impact. The Swedish units represented truly flexible, combined arms formations of integrated infantry and artillery, all with the result of greater mobility and punch.

Tercios, on the other hand, were giant squares designed to either out-muscle or outweigh the opposition with the "push of the pike." Despite the commitment of up to 3000 men per square, only those lining the outside were really useful. The vast majority of men in the tercios stood within the formation, their pikes and muskets pointed to the sky. They had to try to keep step, while waiting for engaged soldiers on the edge to fall so they could replace them. For all its fearsome appearance, tercios were an extravagant waste of manpower. Worse, they were extremely slow and cumbersome. Imagine trying to march around in a 3000-man box formation.

The tercio's greatest vulnerability, however, was from gunpowder weapons, especially artillery. What musket or cannon fire missed on the outside edges inevitably hit someone else as it passed through the densely packed square of humanity. Furthermore, tercios had no organic artillery support of their own. Tilly's cannons were huge pieces requiring dozens of horses, men, and wagons to move them. In short, once Tilly's artillery was employed, it wasn't going anywhere. It lacked tactical mobility, and was altogether a waste of combat power.

Even more important than this was the developed involvement of the subordinate leadership elements of Gustavus' army. It is one thing to have more improved formations. It is an entirely different thing to find capable leaders trustworthy enough to manage those formations. The rapid, sweeping maneuvers at Breitenfeld required a lot of capable subordinate leaders. Because Gustavus spent much of his time in this battle literally in the fog of war, he had to be able to trust all his squadron and brigade commanders, not just Marshals Horn and Baner, to perform the faster-paced and farther-reaching maneuvers.

Gustavus was most proud of his Swedish soldiers, especially the rank and file who must have had nerves of steel to stand fast when the battle was going awry. Under such pressure, they could have broke and run, which was common at the time. (In fact, about half of Tilly's once proud army broke and stampeded away.) But Gustavus' army was unique. All his carefully administered reforms such as regular pay, regular meals, warm uniforms, and rigorous training paid off. He replaced aged or incompetent officers with younger, more capable men. In Gustavus' army, rank was held as much on the basis of merit as on birthright, a radical concept for a seventeenth-century army. His soldiers respected him as a person as well as their leader. They appreciated his concern and commitment to their welfare. In sum, he had ingrained his soldiers with confidence in him, themselves, their leadership, and the army.

Gustavus increased the interdependencies between his army's different elements so they could help each other when needed. Many of his artillery commanders gave up the prestige of gathering around larger cannons and dozens of men, horses, and wagons for the relative Lilliputian three-pound shot regimental cannons. By doing so, the leaders could move cannons with the infantry and provide devastating direct fire support when and where it was needed, unlike Tilly's cannons which sat idle most of the day after the opening barrages.

Gustavus also maximized a principle of integration in the placement of higher ratios of gunpowder weapons into his new, smaller, linear formations, which yielded greater mobility and firepower. He involved more people in the franchise, especially his subordinate leaders who were now invested in the organization and eager to prove their worth to their king who had put his trust in them. His whole army was ingrained with newer methods, expectations, and confidence in themselves and their leadership. Consequently, they hung tough at the bidding of the king even when the battle seemed all but lost. In short, they not only believed in their king, but they believed in their new system. In succeeding years the rest of the European armies began to follow suit and reform in the same manner as Gustavus' army.

What is crucial to any understanding of Gustavus was that he was a brilliant synthesizer of other people's ideas. He knew his Swedish homeland had a small strategic base in terms of manpower and resources. If he were to triumph it would be on the basis of quality, not quantity.

As a young man, Gustavus traveled extensively. In the Netherlands, he met a military leader and theorist, Maurice of Nassau, who advocated different structured formations for better command, control and firepower. It was here that the seed of the future lethal squadrons was sown. Gustavus was also a religious man, committed to the Protestant cause. He had a strong personal faith. His sense of self-worth was not solely based on his monarchy. Compared to other monarchs, Gustavus viewed himself as a servant of the state, unlike other more, arrogant kings of the time.

When it came time to search for ways to break the military status quo of stalemate, Gustavus had the strength of character to listen and defer to other people's better ideas and experience. His ego was not threatened by the enfranchisement of numerous subordinates. The "rank and file" noticed and appreciated his personal integrity and genuine concern for the welfare of those entrusted to him. In the final analysis, it was his character that made success possible. Ironically, Gustavus would die in battle less than a year later, but his army and system triumphed long after his death. He is remembered in history as a "Great Captain" of war who initiated a military revolution.

12 STATUS QUO MUST GO: NAPOLEON

> *"Study the human side of history… to learn that Napoleon in 1796 with 20,000 beat the combined forces of 30,000 by something called economy of force or operating on interior lines is a mere waste of time. If you can understand how a young unknown man inspired a half-starved, ragged, rather Bolshie crowd; how he filled their bellies; how he out-marched, outwitted, out-bluffed and defeated men who had studied war all their lives and waged it according to the textbooks of their time, then you will have learned something worth knowing."*
>
> —SIR ARCHIBALD PERCIVAL WAVELL

THE BLISSFUL ignorance of a prevailing status quo can be wonderful, providing there is nothing that rocks the boat. The U.S. automobile industry before 1972 comes to mind. American car manufacturers blissfully churned out oversized, gas-guzzling "muscle cars" for a huge domestic market where fuel prices seemed negligible. The status quo represented by Detroit assembly lines has much in common with the military parade grounds of eighteenth century Europe, the status quo that the young Napoleon was born into.

In many ways Napoleon Bonaparte was the least likely candidate to lead a great nation to glory. He had the wrong birthplace, spoke the wrong language, and was in the wrong class in seventeenth and eighteenth century European society. But France was soon on the verge of a revolution and he was no ordinary young man. Born the son of lower Corsican nobility on the Mediterranean island of Corsica in 1769, Napoleon's chances of international fame and fortune were slim to none. Unless prepared to settle for a quiet life of obscurity, opportunity on Corsica was less than alluring.

At any rate, his parents decided for him the not too uncommon fate of many sons of lower nobility at that time who happened not to be the first born male. He was earmarked for a career in the Army. At the age of nine, the young boy, who could barely speak French, was shipped off to military boarding school in France. A combination of his thick Corsican accent and the renowned snobbishness of the French left the young boy a bit of a social outcast. Undaunted by rejection from his peers, the energetic young man set himself to becoming a voracious reader and learner. By age sixteen, he had graduated two years early and at the top of his class from the Ecole Militaire in Paris.

Newly commissioned as a Second Lieutenant in the Artillery, Napoleon followed a typical career path as a junior officer, with postings to tactical units. Still, the baggage of being a foreigner, without the necessary social pedigree, continued to plague his career. He was generally excluded from the all-important officers' social scene, which posed a serious problem. One must keep in mind that eighteenth-century European officer corps were comprised almost entirely of nobility. Rank was held on the basis of aristocratic social standing and influence, not merit.

Families of nobility who had sons in the army were usually granted some form of tax exempt status or relief. This was a common way for monarchs to lure and keep excess numbers of bored and over-entitled nobility constructively occupied and out of palace politics. This policy was vital in preserving the all-important status quo for those (monarchs and nobility) on top of the social and political pyramid.

Not prone to worry about things beyond his control, Napoleon instead dedicated himself to leaning his military craft. Unlike his peers, who spent much of their time networking and spending their fortunes at the officer club, he became an exemplary young Lieutenant, both technically and tactically proficient. Unfortunately, despite his obvious talents, the military system of eighteenth century armies limited him to a career in the lower ranks as a junior officer, probably never rising above the grade of Captain.

Napoleon's problem was that European armies of the day were organized along the lines of what military historians refer to as the "Frederican" model. This refers to the Army of the Prussian King, "Frederick the Great," who successfully fought a series of limited wars in the eighteenth century to expand and consolidate the Prussian State. This period was referred to as "The Age of Limited Warfare" because of the severe limitations and restrictions of what armies could do at that time. External and internal factors contributed to this phenomenon.

Outside of the military arena, the Enlightenment dominated the intellectual and philosophical thought of the day. The conclusion of many was that total or unrestricted warfare was a total waste of time and money. Their evidence was the Thirty Years War, which ravaged central Europe at enormous cost of human life and resources. Even more, by the end of it few could even remember what they were fighting over in the first place. War was a risky, costly, and wasteful endeavor that needed to be limited.

Additionally, improved versions of gunpowder weapons such as muskets and artillery now dominated the battlefield. This caused an exponential rise in financial cost and logistical support. Compounding the problem was the proliferation of gunpowder weapons and the continued evolution of corresponding linear tactics. These factors caused a quantum leap in lethality on the battlefield. It was literally possible for a General, if he wasn't very careful, to lose an entire army in a single afternoon. Even victories could be pyrrhic, because of the rapid consumption of material and men that victory would require. Consequently, monarchs usually gave their generals very limited objectives and a host of operational restrictions. Much warfare at this time consisted as much of posturing as actual fighting.

Internally, the Frederican model of armies caused an additional host of limitations and operational problems. Incompetent leadership was foremost. The officer corps of European armies was comprised of nobility, many of which were hopelessly incompetent. A sixteen-year old could very well be a Colonel in charge of a regiment of over a thousand men because of his family name and political affiliation.

Trust and loyalty were also major problems. Because the new gunpowder armies were so expensive and lethal, no king was willing to risk his productive tax base to the fortunes of the battlefield slaughterhouse. Monarchs opted instead to fill the ranks with foreigners and the poor and unfortunate of Europe. Desertion was rampant. Morale and discipline were consistently poor. Simple administrative measures, such as regular pay and food, were often neglected due to corrupt or incompetent officers. Armies were forced to impose stringent disciplinary measures, which only made the men even more resentful. In addition, the large numbers of foreigners only aggravated internal communication problems. By the end of the Seven Years War, the vast majority of Frederick the Great's army did not speak German as a first language.

Most eighteenth century armies actually resembled large mobile prisons, led by officers acting more like prison guards than efficient combat leaders. An army usually traveled together as one large mob so the soldiers could be more efficiently "supervised." The logistical advantage of foraging (scrounging or living off the countryside) was often forfeited for fear that the foraging soldiers would simply run away. Armies, whenever possible, camped in the open and avoided traveling through wooded areas to reduce the temptations of the men to desert. Information was rarely disseminated, not so much for fear of breaches in operational security, but rather that if the locations and routes of march were known to the soldiers, they would conspire more easily to escape. Frederick the Great himself said, "If my men ever began to think not one would remain in the ranks."

Logistically, armies operated on what was known as the "five day tether." Supporting the growing numbers of gunpowder weapons, especially artillery, meant increased need for wagons. This, in turn, caused an exponential rise in the need for

horses. But horses consumed huge amounts of fod-
der. This then required the need for even more
horses and wagons, and so on. Typically, supply officers calculated that that armies could wander five
days away from any pre-positioned supply depot before supplies ran out.

All these external and internal factors added up
to an operational inability to fight or maneuver
boldly or creatively. Because of logistics, trust, and
incompetent subordinate leadership, generals
hesitated before subdividing their armies into
multiple independent maneuver elements (corps).
Forms of maneuver such as turning movements,
sweeping envelopments, and rapid pursuit were
near impossible. For all the money, men, and
resources nations poured into their armed forces,
the relative "product quality" was dreadful. However, it was a status quo not easily revised, especially
by kings and nobility. Unproductive and excessive
members of the nobility were continually steered
out of politics and into the army. Their families
continued to receive tax breaks, enabling them to
maintain their lavish lifestyles and huge estates.
And the kings enjoyed vastly reduced internal
political threats to their thrones. Having to tolerate
some military limitations was a small price to pay to
keep the social order of Europe.

If the monarchs of Europe were willing to sacrifice
efficiency to maintain a beneficial status quo, so too
were the executives at GM, Ford, and Chrysler before

1972. The economy of the huge internal U.S. market was strong. Cheap fuel and non-existent foreign competition left the deck stacked in favor of the U.S. auto giants. We blissfully continued to produce "land yachts" and "muscle cars" noted more for their size and styling than their fuel efficiency and reliability. General long-term product quality even took a back seat to planned obsolescence! But this was a status quo that domestic carmakers and Americans were comfortable with as we all settled into the soft seats and cushy rides of our LTDs and Lincoln Continentals. These cars, like the armies of the eighteenth century, were unwieldy, inefficient, and costly.

The ruling class and nobility of Europe rigged the military systems of the day to preserve their position. So did the auto executives who continued to produce inefficient products in the land of cheap gas. The real needs of the consumer were not the genuine concern. The monarchs and auto executives looked inward, not outward, in fashioning their products whether the "product" was an army or a car. Unfortunately, favorable status quos are too often more fragile and temporary than we would like to believe.

Revolution Abounds

It's odd how seemingly unrelated events can have great repercussions on each other. It has often been said that the shots fired at Lexington and Concord to begin the American Revolution were "heard around the world." France, an ocean away, would for numerous reasons be awakened by that call and enter into its own tumultuous revolution. Similarly, shots fired by an Egyptian army to begin the 1973 Yom Kippur War would have huge repercussions in the U.S. No one could anticipate that the Arab-dominated OPEC (Oil Producing Economic Countries) would initiate a crippling oil embargo on us! Our seemingly invulnerable oil-based economy threatened to come to a screeching halt. Even/odd gas days and long lines at the gas stations were an unimaginable sight in this land of plenty.

For Louis the XV as well as the U.S. auto executives, the status quo was crumbling. Even as the starving mobs were rioting in the streets, Marie Antoinette countered with, "Let them eat cake." Likewise Detroit implored us to "buy American" and continued to produce gas-guzzlers in the face of crisis.

The French king and his ministers blamed bad agricultural crop seasons. The car executives did the same, blaming the unions, the energy crisis, and unfair foreign competition. They had excuses but they didn't have answers. A lifetime of reaping the benefits of a benign but privileged status quo had left them unable to meet the challenge of change. Chrysler was brought to its knees on the verge of bankruptcy. Its CEO, Lee Iacoca, begged the government for a bailout. What did he do with the money? Built "K" cars, more of the same. Not only were both the French monarchy and U.S auto executives approaching bankruptcy, worse, they were out of ideas.

Nature abhors a vacuum. Into the U.S. breech would rush Japanese car manufacturers like Datsun, Honda, and Toyota. Unlike American manufacturers, the Japanese were not out of ideas. QFD, quality function deployment, became their modus operendii. They looked to the ever-changing need of the consumer market to guide them. They would build products that the consumer wanted, not what they thought the consumer should have. They did not dictate to the market. They let the market dictate to them. Survey teams fanned out across the country to ask the American public what they needed in a car. From this information, intelligent decisions could be brought to bear on the design and manufacturing process. The features left in, added or taken out of their cars were based on the rationale of consumer need, functionality, quality, and lower pricing.

As a result, Japanese cars flooded the once impenetrable American market. Car models like Accord, Camry, and 240Z sold like hotcakes. They were fuel-efficient, reliable, longer lasting, and less expensive. There would be more than a decade of decline before U.S. manufacturers could recover and become competitive again. But the cost was high. Their world would never be the same as the Japanese took a huge portion of the American market share.

Into the French breech of revolutionary upheaval rushed ruthless revolutionaries like Robespierre and members of the infamous Committees on Public Safety, who promptly set about consolidating their power through terror. But more importantly, into this breech jumped the young Napoleon.

The winds of change and seething discontent had left the French nobility disenfranchised. Many were rounded up for execution by "Madame guillotine," imprisoned, or forced to flee the country. This posed a real problem for the French Army, which had previously relied upon nobility to fill its officer ranks. Complicating matters was the threat from every major power in Europe, which were mobilizing to crush the upstart French rebellion and restore King Louis to his throne. At the precise time France was surrounded by enemies, the army was rendered "officerless." Where would the new breed of military leadership come from?

The Sword Unsheathed

As the newly promoted Captain Bonaparte was being transferred between assignments, revolution was sweeping the country. Young officers like Napoleon had to choose: either remain a loyalist, or take your chances with the revolutionary cause. Instead of lamenting the collapse of the old order, Napoleon chose to see opportunity. He chose well.

En route from his last assignment, Napoleon stopped at the French port of Toulon. Toulon was the last major Royalist stronghold under siege by revolutionary forces. Napoleon willingly rendered his assistance to the revolutionaries by telling them how to better employ their artillery. His advice made a difference, and the stubborn port soon fell. His evaluation report read, "Words fail me to describe Bonaparte's merits. He has plenty of knowledge, and as much intelligence and courage; and that is no more than a first sketch of a most rare officer." He had been noticed.

At age twenty four, Napoleon was promoted to General and given a garrison command in Paris by his grateful revolutionary government. Yet it wasn't long before the new political masters of France ran things as inefficiently as the old regime. Again rioters took to the streets of Paris. The nervous revolutionary government looked to the young Napoleon to restore order. If he could not, they would be next in line for Madame Guillotine. The revolution hung in the balance.

How Napoleon handled the riot was in keeping with his attitude toward the use of force. To order guns turned on your own people is a particularly distasteful task for any soldier. Nevertheless, Napoleon reasoned that a quick shock effect would be decisive in dispelling the riots and save vastly greater lives in the long run than if the unrest was permitted to grow out of control. He gave the mob "a whiff of grape." Without hesitating, he ordered artillery to fire grapeshot into the unruly crowd. It worked. The word quickly got out that this new regime meant business and order was quickly restored. Later, he commented that "once the sword is out of the scabbard, I shall not sheathe it again until order is restored."

After his success in dispersing the riot, his grateful superiors rewarded him with a large field command in Italy. Napoleon was on his way. From the moment he arrived in Italy, it was no longer business as usual. Upon inspection, he found his new command rife with incompetence, defeatism, and corruption. He quickly sacked incompetent or corrupt officers. He addressed his soldiers directly and committed himself to their welfare. He restored accountability amongst his staff so available food and necessary supplies went to his starving soldiers. His soldiers subsequently responded and out-fought and out-marched the better equipped and more numerous Austrians. His successes in Italy gave him his first taste of notoriety in the new French Republic. In 1799 he successfully parlayed this popularity into a coup d' etat, where he emerged as First Consul. He was now master of France.

More than just a tough general and political leader, Napoleon was open to sweeping reforms and

reorganization of the army. France was still surrounded by enemies. He realized that an effective
French army could not be an incrementally improved version of the prevailing Frederican model.
If France was to survive and expand, its army had to
be much better. Napoleon realized that in order to
secure victory for France, he had to dramatically
change the character of his organization. How did
he do it?

13 CHARACTER VALUES IN ACTION: NAPOLEON

THE REVOLUTION had completely destroyed the old social and political order in France. In the new French Republic, incompetent nobility no longer had a monopoly on the officer corps. Napoleon seized this opportunity to promote new officers from veterans within the ranks. This enabled the French army to actually build competent levels of subordinate leadership from General down to individual platoons.

Napoleon also greatly benefited from the *levee en mass*, Europe's first comprehensive national draft. Because of this, the ranks were now filled with more capable and trustworthy manpower. These citizens were invested in preserving the revolution and defending their country. Duty and patriotism became the principal motivators. In short, Napoleon possessed a distinguishing advantage from other European armies of the day: competent subordinate leadership and reliable, trustworthy soldiers. From this new raw material he fashioned La Grande Armeé, which soon overwhelmed Europe.

The most significant reform Napoleon undertook was reorganizing his army into the "corps system." Basically, this meant subdividing the army into independent multiple maneuver elements called corps. Each corps was comprised of several divisions. Typically, the size of a corps ran anywhere from 20,000 to 30,000 men. With attached artillery, engineers, and cavalry for reconnaissance, each corps was a fully independent and self-sufficient combat organization.

The idea behind the corps system was that the army could spread out, with various corps traveling along multiple avenues of advance, and then rapidly converge to fight. This bold concept had huge operational advantages. First, a trustworthy army that could fan out on the march could more effectively forage, releasing the commanders from the restrictive five-day tether. Second, an army advancing along multiple approaches was extremely confusing to an opponent. Third and most important, this new system allowed for more effective and decisive maneuvering schemes.

While advancing on multiple fronts, one corps would inevitably meet the enemy army. In military terms, this is called a meeting engagement. The engaged corps' job was to "fix" the enemy army and hang on until the other corps converged onto the battlefield. From the enemy's perspective, the converging corps of Napoleon's Grande Armee were the real threat, often arriving unexpectedly from surprising directions. (Remember that the other European armies traveled and fought as one big mob.) The corps system allowed Napoleon to fix his opponent in place with a minimum of force while he swiftly maneuvered the remainder of his forces to the unsuspecting enemy's flanks and rear. Similar to Gustavus' squadrons, but on a much grander scale, Napoleon's corps system could swarm around and annihilate the lumbering leviathan armies of Europe.

Yet the decisive factor for Napoleon's corps system was capable subordinate leadership. Napoleon's army could be spread out over dozens of miles of frontage while on the march. As effective as he was, Napoleon could only be in one place at one time. Standard operating procedure was that the advancing corps were to stay within mutually supporting distance of each other. This was loosely defined as half a day's march. If one corps found and fixed the enemy army, then the other corps would "march to the sound of the guns" and converge onto the battle in a timely manner. As they converged, Napoleon would give them new instructions via messengers on horseback. But messenger communication was often slow and unreliable. Messengers could be shot or captured, arrive too late, or get lost. The corps commanders had to be able to navigate and operate independently themselves when problems arose. In other words, they had to exercise initiative in the absence of orders. It was truly a decentralized command structure, upheld by the quality and trust of subordinate leadership.

Fortunately, Napoleon chose outstanding subordinate leaders as corps commanders. Men such as Marshals Desaix, Devout, Lannes, Berthier, Marmont, Soult and Ney were brilliant commanders who exercised initiative and displayed courage. The corps system was not without risk. If the other converging corps did not arrive in time, then the initial corps fixing the enemy could be destroyed in an outnumbered fight. Time and time again, Napoleon's Marshals came through.

The battle of Marango was one such situation. The Battle of Marango was actually the first trial run of the corps system. It was also a battle that Napoleon needed to win to consolidate his recent political ascendancy as First Consul of France. At that time in May 1800 the Austrians controlled Northern Italy, which earlier had been French territory. To recover Italy for France would be a tremendous victory against the Austrian superpower.

The problem was that Northern Italy, ringed by the Alps, was tough to access, let alone transport armies there. To destroy the Austrian forces in Italy, Napoleon devised a bold and risky plan. His army, subdivided into corps commands, moved through several different Alpine passes in order to confuse Austrian General Michael von Melas.

Knowing that the French were on the move, Melas rushed his army westward towards Turin to intercept what he guessed would be the entire French force emerging through the great St. Bernard Pass. But Napoleon's army emerged through multiple passes, racing eastward and far behind the Austrian army. Melas was stunned, for the French seemed to be everywhere at once. In military terms, the Austrians had been "strategically enveloped." Time worked against Melas. Cut off from his supply line and communication with Austria, Melas was forced to counter-march eastward and fight his way out of Italy before his supplies ran out. He was cut off from his five-day tether and the logistical clock was ticking. He was desperate.

Napoleon had trapped Melas. Now all that remained was to destroy his army. Everything was going as planned or so it seemed. But we have all heard the expression that "the devil is in the details." The French were now to experience some problems of their own, generated by none other than Napoleon himself.

Predictably, Marshal Jean Lannes, one of Napoleon's lead corps commanders, found and fixed the Austrian force just east of Alessandra on what is called the plain of Marango. It was the right time for Napoleon to maneuver Marshal Louis Charles Desiax's converging corps into the battle and finish off Melas. But Napoleon misread the entire situation; he did not realize that Lannes had already locked horns with the entire Austrian force. Incredibly, Napoleon ordered Desiax to march away from the unfolding battle in search of a nonexistent Austrian army.

Desiax could not believe the order. Not having found any other Austrians and operating on a hunch that Napoleon was wrong, Desiax did a smart thing. He slowed, then paused his movement, making sure to remain within mutually supporting distance. In doing so, Desiax retained the option to return to Marango in a timely manner, if and when his boss figured this situation out, and sent a desperate call for help.

By noon, Marshal Auguste Fredereric Marmont's corps had joined Marshal Lannes. It wasn't enough and the two were being ground down by the still numerically superior Melas. Napoleon finally realized he had blundered and sent a frantic message to Desiax. "I had thought to attack Melas. He has attacked me first. For God's sake come up if you still can!"

Marshal Desiax quickly counter-marched his corps and by three o'clock had arrived literally in the nick of time as the French line was about to be broken. Upon arrival onto the battlefield, Desaix himself is said to have stated, "The battle is completely lost, but there is time to win another." The sudden arrival of an entire French corps under

Desaix reversed the battle. Napoleon was able to organize a crushing counterattack. By six o'clock Melas was annihilated. The French had snatched victory from the jaws of defeat. But not without cost, as Marshal Desaix lay among the dead on the grainfields of Marango.

The battle of Marango illustrates the effectiveness of flexibility, agility, teamwork, and initiative in the French army. Even when Napoleon himself had blundered, his organization was able to recover rapidly. The bravery and personal initiative of empowered subordinates operating in a flexible system could overcome the challenges and chaos of battle. The army that Melas commanded simply did not have the operational reach and agility that now characterized the French. Melas could not send independent, coordinated sub-elements of his army on far-reaching sweeping envelopments to cut off enemy lines of communications as Napoleon could. Melas could not spread out forces to deliberately confuse an enemy, as Napoleon could.

Marango had served notice that the old Frederican-style armies were obsolete. The new French corps system, even on a bad day, was still good enough to defeat Melas.

14 A NEW TYPE OF MILITARY CULTURE: NAPOLEON

AFTER MARANGO, Napoleon was convinced he had the correct doctrine, structure, and manpower to form a dominating army. He promptly set about implementing additional reforms to perfect the corps system. At the tactical level (the smaller formations; such as Brigade, Battalion, and Company that make up a larger Division), French soldiers now fought in Demi-brigades. Demi-brigades capitalized on l' Ordre Mixte (open or mixed order) tactics, which offered even greater flexibility and combinations of column, linear, and skirmishing formations. Additionally, medium and light cannons were integrated into the Infantry at a desired ratio of five cannons to 1000 men. At the operational level (a whole field army conducting a battle or campaign), the corps system gave Napoleon and his Marshals flexibility. Demi-brigades gave the Colonels, Majors, and Captains increased flexibility at the tactical level.

Napoleon revamped and professionalized his staff system to better serve the decentralized command structure and insure that his orders and intentions were efficiently communicated. He wanted to be sure to retain positive control over such an inherently flexible instrument. By 1805, the staff of the Imperial headquarters exceeded 400 officers. It was divided into two groups, the Maison and General staff. The Maison was more of a personal staff to assist Napoleon in everything from terrain analysis and intelligence estimates to diplomacy. The general staff, under the capable supervision of Marshal Louis-Alexandre Berthier, tended more to the daily needs and business of supporting and directing the army.

Napoleon also deliberately promoted a new culture for his army. The "Marshallate" became a new kind of aristocracy; an aristocracy of merit. General officers given command of a corps were awarded the rank of Marshal and lavished with benefits and privilege. Many of Napoleon's Marshals had been enlisted soldiers in the old regime. Their promotion to the rank of Marshal sent a clear message that merit was noticed and rewarded in the new regime. It was possible to rise from the lowest rank to the highest. Elite units such as the Old Guard and Imperial Guard were formed. Napoleon also resurrected an old Roman tradition of placing eagles on battle flagstaffs for proven units. He lavished awards on even the lowest ranking soldiers. By doing so, he sent a message to soldiers that their efforts and sacrifices were recognized by the army's leaders, even by Napoleon himself. Their officers were truly concerned for their welfare, a radical concept for an eighteenth century army. This generated proud, trustworthy, and motivated soldiers.

Napoleon had ingrained in his army a new set of core values that promoted bravery, cooperation, dedication, and initiative. He even renamed the French army, calling it the *La Grande Armeé*. And grand it was, compared to the competition.

The Austrians also took stock of their sound thrashing at Marango. Austrian Emperor Francis gave his capable brother, Archduke Charles, the task of studying and reforming the army. The Hofskriegsrat (supreme war council) was established to investigate potential reforms. Archduke Charles knew the Austrian army to be inefficient and obsolete. He recommended numerous reforms such as division and corps structure, opening of the officer ranks to all classes of society, and promotion on merit. In short, he was trying to emulate the French.

It is one thing to identify the necessity for change. It is quite another thing entirely to overcome inertia and the vested interests of the status quo to actually implement change. Remember there had been no revolution in the Austrian Empire. For the monarchy and nobility to open up the officer ranks to all classes of society was in effect a willing sacrifice of their position and power. This they were not prepared to do. Thus, the Austrian army failed to implement the lessons so dearly paid for in blood at Marango. For the Austrians, five years later, it was still business as usual. The obsolete muscle car of the 1970s was about to get another spin around the military block.

Ironically, the lack of initiative within the Austrian army was not as evident in their diplomatic efforts. If the Austrian army was lackluster, Austrian foreign policy was overly ambitious in its desire to seize Bavaria. Austrian ambition collided with French expansion. War between two European superpowers was on its way. Unfortunately for the Austrians, they were about to commit the oldest, most tempting, and most fatal of mistakes. Their external desires and strategy did not match their internal capability to follow through.

At the head of the invading Austrian army was the twenty-five-year old Archduke Ferdinand, who was ill-equipped for high command. Advising the young Archduke was the veteran, yet plodding Chief of Staff Karl Mack. Interestingly, Napoleon knew Mack and had taken him prisoner in the Marango campaign. When Napoleon heard that Mack was to be the de facto Austrian commander, victory became almost guaranteed. Of Mack, Napoleon commented,

> "Mack is a man of the lowest mediocrity I ever saw in my life; he is full of self-sufficiency and conceit, and believes himself equal to anything.

He has no talent. I should like to see him opposed some day to one of our better generals...and, besides all that, he is unlucky."

Since Mack was so predictable, Napoleon's plan
was all the more bold. Shielded by the Rhine River
and the Black Forest, the Grande Armee ap-
proached, then penetrated the northern part of the
Black Forest along multiple axis. As in the Battle of
Marango, Napoleon used large natural terrain features to mask his approach.

Mack's army paralleled the Danube River as it
lumbered westward into Bavaria. He was ignorant
of the forces building up behind the Black Forest,
about to emerge from the northeast. Without accu-
rate information, Mack decided to settle along the
convergence of the Danube and Iller rivers, in the
vicinity of Ulm. Unbeknownst to him, Napoleon's
multiple corps swept through the northern part of
the Black Forest and raced past Mack eastward,
running parallel north of the Danube River. In dramatic fashion, Napoleon's corps wielded south and
settled on the Danube at multiple sites well beyond
Mack's main force, which was still centered around
Ulm. Swiftly Napoleon's corps crossed the Danube
at multiple sites and curled in behind Mack, sever-
ing his line of communication to Austria.

Napoleon had just executed a most rare turning
movement (a daring maneuver in which an army
goes completely around an opponent and swoops

in from behind) considered to be beyond the capability of armies at that time. It was executed so swiftly that Mack was left stunned and paralyzed with confusing reports of the French suddenly everywhere at once. Mack's bottled-up forces were compressed in at Ulm, only to be surrounded and destroyed in what was really a foregone conclusion. In a letter to Josephine, Napoleon wrote, "I have accomplished my objective; I have destroyed the Austrian Army by sheer marching." Once again a plodding army under the obsolete Frederican model was quickly demolished by a new system that moved farther and faster.

Ironically, a common myth about Napoleon is that it was his brilliant battlefield generalship that made him a "great captain" of war. Yet much of Napoleon's greatness can be attributed to the brilliant military system he created. At the decisive battle of Jena/Auerstadt in Prussia, the Grande Armee effectively annihilated the proud Prussian army. Again it was the audacity and initiative he instilled in his corps commanders, especially Marshal Devout, that enabled victory. In fact, it was not until a day or so later that an ignorant Napoleon had fully pieced together what had actually happened and realized the scale of their victory. Historian Owen Connelly picked up on this theme and wrote a book about Napoleon called *Blundering to Glory*.

Napoleon's army was superior because it made much better use of each individual's potential. Like

Gustavus, Napoleon willingly went against the conventional norms of the time and involved more people in the franchise. He intuitively grasped the importance of a level playing field for the people under his command. He did not allow the traditional "walls" of societal norms to stand between people, block their advancement, or promote inefficiency.

With a merit-based model of leadership, replacing the old regime's blatant aristocratic favoritism, a sense of integrity and legitimacy was restored to the army as an institution. This then insured the best involvement of the best people. The ingraining of new values and expectations dramatically improved motivation and trust throughout the ranks. New organizational structures (the corps system) and operational doctrines (bold maneuver schemes) stressed teamwork, initiative, and stronger interdependencies. The Grande Armee became a much faster, more flexible, and lethal instrument.

15 A FALL FROM GRACE: NAPOLEON

ON DECEMBER 2, 1804, Napoleon had himself crowned Emperor. The French Republic, born of the revolution, now took on all the trappings of an imperialist empire. The constitution was amended to state, "The government is entrusted to an hereditary emperor." Bonaparte was now Napoleon I. France had replaced one monarch, Louis XVI, with another, Napoleon I.

After the Ulm Campaign, Napoleon would go on to win a series of spectacular battlefield successes. Decisive victories at Austerlitz and Jena Auerstadt made him master of central Europe. His Grand Armee was unbeatable. As his successes and conquests grew, however, so did his ambition and pride. For Napoleon, it was no longer enough to have hegemony over Europe. He wanted complete, unilateral dominance over all Europe, including England and Russia.

Unfortunately for Napoleon, the English Channel and Lord Horatio Nelson's brilliant Admiralship stood between England and the Grande Armee. Unable to bring England to her knees in a military conquest, Napoleon sought to do it economically through the "Continental System." Essentially, all European ports were to be closed to English merchant ships, forcing this nation of shopkeepers to starve for goods.

In theory, the continental system seemed like a good idea. However, as things often do, the plan broke down in the details. Portugal, on the western edge of the Iberian Peninsula, still actively traded with England. Additionally, England already had a worldwide market in her colonies outside of Europe. For England, loss of European trade, though hard, was by no means crippling.

Nevertheless, Napoleon took action to close the Portuguese ports, but geography was a problem. Without sea power, Napoleon's land army had to cross all of Spain just to get to Portugal in order to enforce the ban on English trade. Spain was a non-threatening, neutral country, poor and long past its power on the international scene. Had Napoleon respected Spanish sovereignty and been respectful to the still proud Spanish monarchy, the transit of his armies would have been easy and uneventful. Unfortunately, this was not the new emperor's way. His army behaved more like a heavy-handed occupation force than an army in transit. He humiliated the Spanish royal family through a combination of brow-beatings and undignified bribery. These actions engendered Spanish resentment. As a further affront to the Spanish people, Napoleon sacked the Spanish King and put his own older brother, Joseph, on the Spanish throne.

Soon cries of "Death to the French!" resounded throughout the country, and a guerilla-style "people's war" erupted. Eventually, Napoleon would pour over 300,000 men into the Iberian Peninsula in an attempt to close Portuguese ports and subdue Spain. What began as a limited objective to close Portuguese harbors grew into a Vietnam-style quagmire for France. The English, of course, willingly intervened to help Portugal and Spain. Under the command of Wellington, an English expeditionary force landed and was operating on the continent. This now guaranteed a two front war for Napoleon whenever he again campaigned in central Europe or further east.

Spain was never subdued. It remained for Napoleon "the Spanish ulcer," which siphoned off manpower and resources at a moment when he could ill afford either. And for what? Even if the Portuguese ports were closed with a minimum of French military force, it wouldn't have been devastating to England's commercial prospects. Because of his growing selfishness, Napoleon continued to pursue a useless objective to ridiculous ends. He made enemies out of friends. He frittered away thousands of men, men who could have served the Grande Armee in ways much better than subduing Spanish civilians in an attempt to quell a national insurrection.

Frustrated, the emperor turned east to Russia, the other non-participant in his continental system. In Napoleon's mind there was not enough room on the continent for two empires (his own and Russia's). As with Spain, he picked an unnecessary fight with Tzar Alexander. His massive Grande Armee crossed the Nieman River on June 22, 1812, and the invasion of Russia had begun.

There are many misconceptions about Napoleon's invasion of Russia, the biggest being his actual intent. Never in any of his plans did Napoleon envision marching all the way to Moscow. His plan was to trap and annihilate the Russian army somewhere in what is now modern-day eastern Poland and western Russia. Using his proven superior corps system, he would seek a decisive summer battle, then dictate terms to the Tzar. Going all the way to Moscow was not the strategy.

The Russians, under the brilliant leadership of the old, wise, one-eyed General Mikhail Kutusov, refused to give battle. Kutusov knew he could never lock horns with the Grande Armee and survive. A stinging previous defeat at Austerlitz had taught him that bitter lesson. Consequently, he elected a strategy of evasion and withdrew into the deep interior of Russia. He would let the remorseless elements of "strategic consumption" (loss of combat power due to weather, lack of supplies, fatigue, sickness etc.) wear down the Grande Armee.

Ironically, Napoleon's army was too big for the task. Numbering over half a million men and requiring massive resupply, it moved slowly, more of a bludgeon than a rapier. He could chase but not catch Kutusov. Compounding the effects of Kutusov's withdrawal was the "scorched earth" (the willing destruction of anything useful in the invader's path) policy the Russians pursued.

Before Napoleon realized it, he was at the gates of Smolensk, deep inside Russia. It was already August 12. Fall was fast approaching and he was down to 200,000 men. Without fighting any major battles, over half his army had become casualties to sickness, water shortages, and lack of supplies. He pressed on to Moscow only to find the capital burned and abandoned. Now he was mired deep inside Russia with winter fast approaching, in a burned city that could not support his army. With no other choice, he retreated out of Russia during the merciless winter. Kutusov's Army herded the Grande Armee out the same way it came in. The retreat was a death march in the depths of winter. The once great Grande Armee recrossed the Nieman River with less than seven thousand men. Over 90% of Napoleon's original invasion force did not survive. Nor would his regime.

Russia and Spain proved Napoleon could be beaten. England, Russia, Prussia, and Austria would form coalitions to eventually overwhelm him. Bitter lessons of previous defeats had finally caused the coalition armies to reform themselves along the lines of the French army. They had closed the operational gap.

Just as the European armies would take a decade to catch up to Napoleon, so too would the American car-makers take a decade to compete with Japan. In a strange twist of fate, most of Japan's initial manufacturing and organizational successes were actually based on American ideas. These ideas were first published but went unheeded in America! The Japanese were not original; they were, however, courageous and motivated enough to implement other's innovative ideas.

Likewise with Napoleon. All the innovative military reforms he instituted into the Grande Armee had been thought out and published by the time he was an infant, but there had been no motivation to enact those ideas. Only when history presented the intersection of the French Revolution and Napoleon's maturation and opportunism did these innovative ideas find their time to bloom.

After his debacle in Russia, Napoleon scrambled to reconstitute his army while huge coalition forces were gathering against him. In June of 1813, Napoleon met with Europe's foremost diplomat, the Austrian Count Von Metternich. Metternich could foresee Napoleon's fate and offered him peace if Napoleon would withdraw to France's natural boundaries. In this way, a blood-soaked fight to the finish could be avoided and Napoleon could remain in power. Yet Napoleon would have none of it. "My domination will not survive the day when I cease to be strong and therefore feared." What a telling comment! The man who once lead through positive involvement and inspiration now resorted to the ingraining of domination and fear to keep his hold on power. Knowing that Napoleon had just committed France to slow and bloody death because of his own ego, Metternich responded, "Sire, you are a lost man."

The end would come in a Belgian bean field at a place called Waterloo. Ironically, Napoleon would lose this battle in fashion similar to how the Austrians had lost years before at Marango. At the height of combat, pacing nervously, he fretted over where Marshal Grouchy was: one of his corps commanders he desperately needed to tip the balance. Instead, the allied General Gebhard Blucher's corps of vengeful Prussians arrived in the nick of time to drive into Napoleon's rear and secure victory for Wellington. It is simplistic to note that what comes around often goes around. For Napoleon, forgetting the qualities and character that made him a leader meant that he would once again have nothing.

During his career, Napoleon won the vast majority of battles he fought. Those he did not win were usually tactical draws. Opposing generals feared him and felt his presence alone was worth another 60,000 men. Despite all his battlefield successes, however, he lost in the end because he lost the war within himself. Perhaps his most revealing comment was,

> "I have only one passion, only one mistress, and that is France. She has never failed me, she has lavished her blood and treasures on me. If I need five hundred thousand men, she gives them to me."

The egotism that laced his comment is astounding though a bit misleading. France was Napoleon's mistress, but pride was his first passion. And like most arrogant men, he selfishly indulged in his mistress as an instrument for his own pleasure and vanity. And just as a mistress can be plundered, so too can she be abandoned. It was insanity to march deep into Russia with winter approaching, risking his men to starvation and cold. But at that point Napoleon was thinking less about the welfare of his men and more about the vainglory of bringing a rival emperor to heel.

All the dynamic leadership and character attributes of Napoleon that built his earlier success were later subverted by his own character flaws. Pride and arrogance not only brought down a man but a mighty army and empire as well. In the final analysis his selfishness left his beloved France out in the cold just as he had done to thousands of his soldiers in Russia. A lost war. A lost cause. A lost soul.

It is not enough to develop character in your

organization and then walk away assuming every-thing will always run smoothly. Napoleon assumed that the perfect military system he had built would always work for him because he thought that he mattered more than the values he had imparted.

Creating character is an ongoing, never-ending pursuit. The goal is always to have the whole be more than the mere sum of the parts. Napoleon be-lieved himself to be greater than the organization he had built — a fatal mistake. We can always change ourselves or our organizations. And once changed, we can easily forget from whence we came.

Be strong. Character takes time and patience.

16 THE DISCARDED VICTOR: DOWDING

"I sought for a man... who would... stand in the gap before me on behalf of the land"

—EZEKIEL, SON OF BUZI

IN THIS century, against overwhelming odds, one of western civilization's most crucial battles was fought in 1940. A battle won not because of superior numbers, technology, or tactics. But a battle was won on the basis of superior character, and specifically, the superior character of one man. How did this happen?

Standing in the gap can be as lonely as it is difficult. For it is by definition a solitary task. The fact that a gap or void exists implies previous failure, defeat, or abandonment by others. Filling the void means sometimes standing alone performing a task no one else can or wants to do.

In the summer of 1940, never had the gap yawned so wide. Yet one man would boldly and humbly stand in the gap and win against all odds in what is perhaps one of history's most crucial battles. Ironically, for all his brilliant and valiant efforts, this hero was unceremoniously cast aside after the battle. It would be years before his vital contribution was fully recognized. His name was Air Chief Marshal Hugh Dowding and the gap he stood in was the Battle of Britain in World War II.

By June of 1940, the Nazi juggernaut had become the undefeated master of continental Europe. The German war machine had produced Blitzkrieg (Lightning war) that crushed everything before it in a rapid and shocking manner. A weakened and fragile Britain was left the lone combatant. The only thing that stood between Britain and sure defeat was the English Channel. Fortunately, the German Herrenvolk (master race) could not walk on water. The narrow channel was just enough of an obstacle to temporarily halt the advance of Hitler's unbeatable new Panzer divisions. But the Germans were working steadily to overcome this obstacle.

To launch a cross-channel invasion, the Germans needed to secure safe sea passage, which meant that the Germans had to possess air supremacy. German air supremacy over southern England would keep the British Home Fleet from disrupting the cross-channel invasion. If the Germans could safely put ashore their potent Wehrmacht (army or armed forces), the subsequent land conquest would probably be an easier task than the channel crossing.

In June 1940 Britain was reeling. A large portion of her army was committed overseas defending the empire. The remainder was dribbling in from a desperate evacuation following humiliating defeat in France. Worse, the surviving British Army had been forced to abandon all its heavy equipment and weapons in France. They were in no position to beat back a determined land assault. In an effort to rally his beleaguered nation, Prime Minister Winston Churchill went on national radio and said with absolute sincerity that all the British had to offer was blood, sweat, and toil.

Everything would turn on the coming air battle. If the German Luftwaffe (air force) could sweep the Royal Air Force (RAF), from the skies of southern England, Operation Sea Lion, the German invasion, could go forth. In order to do this the Germans amassed the greatest air fleet ever, more than 2500 top-line aircraft with seasoned aircrews, mobilized to pound southern England.

Leading the RAF Fighter Command against this powerful German force was Air Chief Marshal Hugh Dowding. Distressingly, Fighter Command was much more formidable on paper than in reality. Though numbering approximately 1000 fighters and pilots on paper, the RAF suffered from a decisive lack of experienced pilots. Only half were experienced veterans. An aircraft can be made in a week;

it takes a year to fully train the pilot. Even then, there is a great gulf between the recent flight school graduate and a seasoned veteran. This would be a battle where you had to fight with what you had on hand because the replacements took too long. The true combat ratio facing British fighter pilots was closer to five to one.

Dowding's problems were compounded by the vital necessity of preserving his combat strength. If the Germans ever ran an invasion fleet across the channel, the British Fighter Command had to still have enough strength to provide the British Navy air cover from the Luftwaffe. Dowding could not afford heavy losses. Attrition was his real enemy. Operating at even the most optimistic kill ratios of three to one, what point would there be if there were no pilots left to protect the Navy? In theory, even at a favorable three to one kill ratio, Fighter Command could quickly cease to exist, leaving the Germans with a thousand remaining aircraft in total command of the air. This was an excruciatingly difficult strategic conundrum that few understood and even fewer could solve. Never before since the Spanish Armada of 1588 had Britain been so perilously exposed, and her shores naked to invasion. To think that the fate of western civilization rested on Dowding's Lilliputian force of thousand men is staggering.

For Dowding the Battle of Britain had really begun many years earlier. His first significant appointment was "Air Member for Supply and Research" within Fighter Command of the RAF. This was not a prestigious assignment. During the 1930s, heavy bombers were considered the most important element of an air force, consequently accounting for much of the budget. Strategic bombing dominated air theory and doctrine. In the years between WWI and WWII, air theorists like Giulio Douhet confidently proclaimed that "the bomber will always get through." At the time they were right. There was no reliable way to find and intercept approaching air fleets that were coming from all possible directions and altitudes. Air interception was like trying to find a needle in a haystack. An assignment at Fighter Command did not offer a shot at glory.

The lean inter-war years were extremely frustrating for men like Dowding. Post-World War I demobilization shrunk armies and budgets to a fraction of their former size. Vast air fleets and navies were carted off to their respective junkyards. And yet, the world was on the threshold of a technological revolution. There were many promising new technologies in their infancy that held great promise for aviation and air defense: electronics, radar, and radio communications. Yet men like Dowding were relegated to the sidelines due to a lack of funds.

If the distribution of funds can indicate importance, then the British national defense budget said it all. Even in the 1930s the entire RAF only received 17% of the national defense budget. Of that already thin slice, Fighter Command received only a fraction. Upon retrospect, it seems ironic that the defense of an entire nation would hang on a mere 1% of the total defense budget. Though his position was immensely risky and frustrating, Dowding was not deterred. He grasped the potential of new technologies, especially radar. If proven workable, radar would be the key to the interception problem. The technology was there, but the battle of budgets and perceptions remained.

New technologies implied new priorities and doctrines, which understandably threatened the old guard of trench generals and dreadnought admirals, who were suspicious of "new-fangled" scientific innovations. Liddel Hart, Britain's foremost military theorist, summed it up best, "The only thing harder than getting a new idea in is getting the old ideas out." At one point, funding for technological development was so paltry that Dowding went outside of government channels. He even asked an old wealthy dowager for a large financial grant. This helped keep critical radar research going.

Dowding continued to push for funding and expanded research. At Bawdsey Manner, a large country estate on the coast of Suffolk, he brought together a group of scientists and military staff. Nicknamed the "Bawdsey Soviets," under Dowding's direction they developed the world's first comprehensive radar detection air defense system. Dowding's efforts modeled today's methods of successfully blending research and development with systems integration and organizational effectiveness.

Dowding was also an outspoken advocate of the all-metal single-winged fighters. He relentlessly pushed for the development of promising new aircraft designs such as the Hawker Hurricane and Spitfire. Additionally, bulletproof glass was a recent American development that could easily be obtained on the open market for cockpit canopies. Yet initial funding requests were denied. Dowding was incensed that Chigaco gangsters could ride around behind bulletproof glass, but not his fighter pilots. He continued to aggressively push for further funding. In doing so he made as many enemies as friends.

In 1936 the Air Ministry appointed Dowding head of Fighter Command, a seemingly prestigious promotion. Because of his dour personality and his penchant for sticking to regulations, he had earned the nickname "Old Stuffy." Some insiders had concluded that Old Stuffy was being put out to pasture in a fledgling branch of the British military. Unpopular and frustrated, Dowding could have coasted to retirement; everyone else seemed to be doing just that. Despite gathering clouds of a rearming Nazi Germany, British politicians had not made a move to "stand in the gap." Instead, they opted to pursue appeasement policies to hopefully slow Hitler's spreading aggression and evil. Yet it was not in Dowding's nature to appease an enemy or walk away from challenge, particularly when his country was in such great need.

"Service and Manners"

Born in 1882, the son of a schoolmaster and grandson of a clergyman, Dowding was reared in the classic English boarding school tradition. In today's educational climate that stresses self-esteem and self-fulfillment, demanding boarding school regimes would seem very foreign. Yet for all their rough edges, English boarding schools produced generations of men who subsequently conquered and governed almost one forth of the globe. These schools were known for their first rate education, Spartan environment, discipline, and character development. Their job was to turn sons of the privileged upper crust into men who could assume the mantles of leadership and responsibility in leading the nation.

Dowding's school, Winchester, held as its motto "Service and Manners." In this motto two ideas were firmly ingrained into the young Dowding. First, Dowding was taught to value service and sacrifice to "God, King and Country." Second, "manners" — meaning proper self-conduct and inte-grity were absolutely essential. Simply put, manners were synonymous with good character.

It is often true that people choose careers as a result of the things they try to avoid. Dowding was no exception. He would fall into a military track by default simply because "joining the Army class was the only way I could escape having to learn Greek."

Commissioned at age eighteen as a Second Lieutenant in the Artillery, Dowding's early career path was undistinguished, with postings all over the empire. What he liked most was getting away from the stifling influence of the brass. Though intellectually Dowding was accepting of the conservative traditions of the army, he was not held captive by these traditions. He was a free thinker who had no trouble voicing his opinions. At a staff school assignment he commented, "I was always irked by the lip service the staff paid the freedom of thought, contrasted with the actual tendency to repress all but conventional ideas." This seemingly maverick attitude is usually not well received in a military culture. But Dowding was not so much a maverick as he was committed to intellectual honesty and integrity. There is a fine line between honest intellectual dissent and insubordination. Dowding knew that line and never crossed it.

Knowing his personal traits, Dowding did a smart thing as a junior officer and left the artillery for the romance of the new field of aviation. At the outbreak of World War I, he was one of the few qualified officer pilots. As expected, his career took off. His firm belief in service, personal integrity, and character, combined with his ability to think creatively actually made him an ideal candidate to lead Fighter Command.

The late 1930s had seen the infamous "volunteer" German Legion Condor (deployed to support the Fascists in Spain) terrorize Spain during the Spanish Civil War. It was here that the world got its first glimpse of the horror of strategic bombing. The Spanish City of Guernica was leveled and the world was shocked. This put new pressure on Dowding to knit Fighter Command into an air defense interception network. Luckily for Britain, Dowding's "Bawdsey Soviets" had laid the blueprint for a successful air defense. By the summer of 1940, just in the nick of time, construction had been completed on the world's first integrated radar-directed air defense system, which could effectively vector fighters to interception.

Vision must always accompany invention. The Germans had also developed radar but had not thought to use it for interception purposes, only for fire direction on individual cannons. Dowding's brilliance was in the application of radar for air defense.

17 LET HISTORY JUDGE: DOWDING

DOWDING'S BIGGEST problem remained. He was still was short on fighters. The radar interception became even more crucial as a "combat multiplier," allowing for a much more efficient usage of fewer aircraft. Yet there were still not enough pilots. In June Britain was still well below their calculated projection of 52 full-strength Fighter squadrons needed to defend the home islands.

Churchill and his cabinet were still absorbed in the unfolding defeat in France. Churchill was under extreme pressure from French Prime Minister Reynaud to not abandon but further reinforce France in her hour of need. Dowding knew that further reinforcement with precious fighter squadrons might be a grand gesture to France, but a military waste for Britain. He pleaded not to send any more squadrons to France. France was lost and it was time to face reality by preserving precious strength for the coming German onslaught. Though Dowding was absolutely correct, his message was political suicide. The Prime Minister had to publicly stand by France, and though the decision to abandon France was a military necessity, it was accompanied by huge political risk. Everybody knew that Dowding was correct, but wouldn't admit it or act on it. Even Dowding's superiors in the Air Ministry shrunk away from the heated debate. They left Dowding alone to bear the unpopular message. Dowding's personal courage in conveying a difficult message only earned him the enmity of Churchill and his Cabinet.

After the last British soldier withdrew from Dunkirk, Dowding began to nurse Fighter Command back to strength. Even by late June they were still well below the projected minimal needs. Morale was also a factor. The British Expeditionary Force had been run out of France. Everyone was blaming everyone else for the defeat. The RAF as a whole had done particularly poorly, having lost two-thirds of its aircraft since the war's beginning against the vaunted Luftwaffe. The RAF, especially Fighter Command, was said to have done an ineffective job providing air cover during the Dunkirk evacuation. Dowding's once-famous fighter pilots now came under severe criticism. With low morale and a fledgling air defense system, Dowding was operating under razor-thin margins.

The battle began modestly in mid-July, mostly with probing, intelligence gathering, and limited objectives on the part of the Germans. British aircraft and particularly pilot losses were already alarming. As early as July 19, statistical projections showed that British Fighter Command would cease to exist in six weeks at the current rate of consumption.

Dowding correctly concluded that the number one priority of Fighter Command was survival, a priority even overriding inflicting casualties on the Germans. Attrition was his worst enemy. Knowing the full fury of the German attack was still to come in August, he was in a horrible dilemma. Not to fight was to leave southern England, his airfields, maintenance, and air defense infrastructure open to annihilation. Yet to fully engage risked losing the battle through attrition.

To commit larger numbers in "big wings" (massed squadrons) might kill more Germans but would also be guaranteed to accelerate the attrition of Fighter Command. "Big wing" employment was unacceptable. Dowding's solution instead was to employ "penny packets," the controlled commitment of absolute minimum numbers of fighters to engagements. In this way the bleeding could be slowed.

The penny packet concept was highly unpopular and controversial at the time. This strategy doomed drastically outnumbered line pilots to fly every day into the oncoming fray of huge German air armadas. Pilots would do this up to five and six times a day! An individual fighter pilot's life expectancy in a hopeless statistical situation as this was almost negligible. To their great credit they continued to take to the skies and fight ferociously.

Much has been written about the glory and romance of air combat. At the time, the British media adorned the fighter pilots as knights of the sky. Churchill referred to them as his young "chicks." The reality was completely different. The stress on line pilots was almost unbearable. There are accounts of pilots gagging into their oxygen masks in unsuccessful efforts to literally choke back the fear while forcing themselves to fly into the maelstrom of death.

At this critical juncture two influential pilots, Group Leader Leigh Mallory and a national hero, Squadron Leader Douglas Bader, voiced public opposition to Dowding's penny packet strategy. They advocated the use of big wings. Difference of opinion is not necessarily bad and can be tolerated to a certain degree. But at certain points, particularly in war, unity becomes much more important. As well meaning as Leigh Mallory and Douglas Bader were, their actions bordered on, then crossed the line of insubordination. They wrongfully sparked an unnecessary internal squabble throughout the Air Ministry and the Cabinet, a severe distraction from the fighting in progress. Again Dowding came under intense fire for his management of the battle.

In mid-August came the full fury of the German attack. The German strategy was to destroy Fighter Command's ground infrastructure while luring the

British fighters into larger air battles in an attempt to slaughter them in the sky. By late August the German strategy had begun to work. In the first week in September, RAF Fighter Command was approaching what statisticians refer to as "catastrophic failure." For military organizations this is the point where losses are so heavy that practical function is negated. The battle was climaxing. British intelligence knew that the Germans had tentatively set the invasion date for September 20, and Operation Sea Lion had already been set in motion with the assembly of the invasion fleet. For the next two weeks the free world teetered on the brink of the abyss.

But Dowding persevered. He ignored the critics and stayed the course. With invasion imminent, now more than ever Fighter Command had to remain a viable entity. Precious remaining strength could not be squandered in single grand aerial engagements.

Fortunately for Britain, the Germans almost inexplicably shifted strategy. They went after London itself. This allowed invaluable breathing space for Fighter Command and its infrastructure to recover. It wasn't long, however, before the public began to demand more fighters be committed in defense of the nation's capital. Dowding resisted and stayed the course. London would have to absorb the blows so Fighter Command could remain effective when the German invasion came. Again, an unpopular but correct decision. At this time, Dowding's supporters were decidedly few. The pressure on him to deviate from his strategy was enormous. Dowding would later comment, "Always I am dragged back into the strain when I was fighting the Germans and the French and the Cabinet and the Air Ministry and now and again the Navy for good measure."

The German shift in strategy was disastrous for the Luftwaffe. Militarily, bombing London got them nowhere. In fact, it increased their own operational problems. The extended flight time to London was barely within reach of their own BF 109 Fighter escorts which could only linger for a few minutes before having to return home. In an air supremacy battle, this was at cross-purposes to the original goal to destroy Fighter Command in the air and on the ground. The battle climaxed in the middle of September with Fighter Command still very much in the fray. The Germans thought that the RAF had been destroyed, and were dismayed and demoralized at the continuing presence of swarming British fighters. Even Hitler grudgingly admitted on September 14 that the necessary air supremacy had not been attained. Operation Sea Lion was postponed. Because of deteriorating weather conditions in the channel, the indefinite postponement was a de facto cancellation. Britain was saved.

The battle would rage throughout the rest of the fall with the Germans switching again to night bombing of British cities. Though Britain still endured terror from the night skies, the more deadly threat of invasion had passed. Dowding emerged victorious. His Fighter Command had fought ferociously against daunting odds. More importantly, he had kept his paltry force viable until late September, when the weather conditions in the channel precluded an invasion.

Soon after the battle all of Dowding's political enemies attacked. He came under vicious personal and professional criticism for his conduct of the battle. The penny packet versus big wing debate was resurrected. Politicians like Churchill remembered their loss of face in the bitter debate over reinforcing France. Dowding was fired. In a terse telegram, he was unceremoniously relieved of command and sent on an extended tour of American factories. Shortly thereafter he was forcibly retired on short notice without fanfare. For all his success and genius, he was humiliated and cast aside in what amounted to an inside "palace coup" lead by Leigh Mallory. Upon reflection, a loyal subordinate, Squadron Leader "Ginger" Lacey, best summed up Dowding's unfair treatment, " I cannot understand how the authorities were able to talk about the fate of civilization hanging on the outcome of The Battle of Britain, and yet so easily discard the victor."

To Dowding's great credit, he never went public with his anger or bitter disappointment. Even though the critics failed to conduct themselves with "manners," he would not stoop to their level. With the danger to England's shores passed, he could now fade away and let history judge his actions.

The Battle of Britain is considered one of the most crucial in the history of western civilization. If the battle was lost, Hitler's evil regime would have fully conquered Europe and the history books would read very differently. Historians cite four crucial elements to Britain's victory, all directly attributable to Dowding. First, the crucial technologies of radar and advanced metal fighters were developed under Dowding. Second was Dowding's genius for systems integration in creating the world's first modern air defense network that was unparalleled. As a leader he had turned thought and theory into action and practical application. Third, his courage to stand up to Churchill before the battle to make the unpopular case to cut off air power reinforcement of France was crucial. It prevented Britain from wasting precious strength. Fourth, his judicious husbanding of strength through the policy of penny packets slowed the attrition, allowing Fighter Command to stay in the game just barely long enough to survive. This last decision has been exhaustively studied by historians, computer analysts, and statisticians. Their overwhelming conclusion is that Dowding's policy was the only possible solution to the strategic dilemma. Any earlier deviation from it would have resulted in Britain prematurely running out of pilots, then aircraft, and making Operation Sea Lion possible.

In retrospect, Dowding accomplished far more than anyone could have expected. The tremendous added value he pulled out of the scarce resources of money, manpower, and aircraft is astounding. Iron-ically, the man nicknamed Old Stuffy, for his strict adherence to regulations, was the visionary able to think outside of the box in knitting together a host of infant technologies to create the first air defense system. Additionally, Dowding alone could see the single, though unpopular, strategic solution, even though this solution defied the popular conven-tional wisdom. Dowding exercised perseverance and personal courage in seeing his vision through. His leadership qualities are worth noting. Squadron Leader Lacey bluntly put it well: "Where would we have been if Stuffy had lost the battle?"

In the final analysis The Battle of Britain was won on character as much as by technology, num-bers, or tactics. Victory demanded the character of a man to persevere in the lean times, the character to stand up and do the right thing even if it risked the wrath of a Prime Minister. Victory demanded the character to pursue the harder right over the easier wrong while under the stress of battle and cacoph-ony of stinging criticism. Character meant not stooping to the level of critics.

Contrast Dowding's character with the actions and motivations of the enemy leadership. As men-tioned earlier, as of September 7, the Luftwaffe seemingly inexplicably shifted targets from Britain's defense infrastructure to London. Why? The an-swer lies in character, or rather a complete lack of it.

Until this point in WW II, strategic bombing of

an enemy's capital was an informal taboo tacitly respected by both sides. But days earlier, more through chance, a disoriented German bomber had inadvertently dropped his bombs in the heart of London. Britain immediately responded with a very small and limited night raid on Berlin that caused negligible damage. Britain's intent was to warn Germany not to bomb London again. Though many would have seen the pinprick reprisal for what it was, the Nazis did not.

In Hitler, Goering, Goebbels, and Himmler, Germany was under the leadership of men who were of a criminal element, men without character. Not surprisingly, when a criminal is confronted, he overreacts. The reaction is usually irrational, immoral, thoughtlessly cruel, or violent. When Berlin was bombed, Hitler went ballistic. The next day he gave a speech at the large Berlin sport palace ranting and raving about revenge. Soon thereafter began the all-out bombing of London.

The German switch in strategy did not make any sense in an air supremacy battle. In fact, it abandoned a working strategy on the verge of success. Dowding and his staff were bewildered. But viewed from the German perspective under Hitler's criminal mindset, it made perfect sense. Impulsiveness and revenge temporarily superceded a well thought-out objective and strategy.

In the end it was Dowding's character in his own camp and the void of it in the German camp that tilted the balance toward Britain. Dowding's biographer, Robert Wright, refers to him as a "practical airman and idealist" but more importantly a man of "simple faith and integrity." Raised in an Anglican religious faith and educated in the tradition of "Service and Manners," Dowding had a personal faith and character that served his nation and indeed the world beyond measure. All his intelligence and gifts would have meant little if he did not have faith and character to guide him.

Among the ancient Greeks, Aristotle stressed that education was to make us better, not necessarily smarter. The imparting of knowledge on our youth is not as crucial as their character development. Ironically, the man who avoided Greek classes makes Aristotle's point. The simple motto of "Service and Manners" of the little boarding school in Winchester had a long reach indeed. The service provided at a time of peril by a man who stood in the gap was incalculable. And it is in the service itself that is the reward. No one knew this better than Dowding himself, the discarded victor.

18 A TRUE REVOLUTIONARY: NGUYEN THI DINH

IN 1966, in a speech to a large political gathering in Hanoi, North Vietnam, Ho Chi Minh stated,

> "The Deputy Commander of the Liberation Armed Forces is Miss Nguyen Thi Dinh. Our country alone in the whole world has such a woman general. This is a glorious thing for the South and for our entire nation."

Ho Chi Minh was pronouncing to the world that the number two official in charge of prosecuting the war in South Vietnam was a woman! This was a stunning revelation, even more pronounced, as the war was rapidly escalating with the massive intervention of America.

In this book, we have used examples of "traditional" historical figures. The disenfranchised of this world can fairly argue that the success of men such as Gustavus Adolphus, Napoleon, or Dowding is predictable, even expected. After all, these men were born high into the power structures of their day. They were not starting from scratch. They were benefactors of the best education available and near or at the top in class structure. They had inherent authority. At their disposal were resources of powerful nations. In a sense their challenge was merely to reorganize the already existing powerful structures around them. They already had a tremendous amount going for them before they met their destinies.

In stark contrast stands a woman, Senior General Nguyen Thi Dinh, the most unlikely of candidates. Born in 1920 to a poor peasant family in the Ben Tre province in the Mekong delta just south of Saigon, she was the youngest of ten children, referred to by their mother as a "flock of ten blackbirds." Nguyen Thi Dinh was a sickly child suffering from asthma. Like her brothers and sisters she had to work hard for the family's survival. By age ten, she would rise at three in the morning to help row a sampan boat laden with fish to a market six miles away. As a young girl, she harbored no ambitions for greatness or national prominence. Yet, though Dinh was a poor peasant's daughter living in the backwater of an underdeveloped country, she would rise to the rank of a Senior General, occupying one of the highest military positions then available among the communist forces operating in South Vietnam. Her successful leadership was instrumental in the struggle to prevail over France and the American superpower. In the story of this humble woman's remarkable life lies the story of communist victory over both France and the United States.

Nguyen Thi Dinh's life and spectacular career demonstrate how ingrained character values combined with moral and physical courage can contribute to victory in the struggle for dignity for one's self, a people and a nation. As a woman, her character added to her determination to overcome societies' tradition-bound obstacles to pursue a greater good. In a very real sense she would be crucial in redefining the norms of a society, while at the same time helping her country achieve independence and unity.

Nguyen Thi Dinh was born into a world that held little hope for her. Her chances of rising above the toil and grinding poverty she and her family experienced daily were slim. Vietnam was then a French colony. Despite pious French claims of "civilizing" a poor, underdeveloped nation, the French shamelessly exploited the people and resources of Vietnam.

In fact this was not always the fate of Vietnam. President Franklin Roosevelt had been adamant about blocking the French return to their colonies in Indochina after the end of WWII. In his view, we

had not fought the war in the Pacific only to rein-
state oppressive imperial European colonialism,
especially that of the French. Much like President
Woodrow Wilson two decades earlier, Roosevelt
envisioned the Vietnamese pursuing self-determin-
ism towards independence and nationhood. His
Administration even used the Office of Strategic
Services (OSS) to support an obscure resistance
group lead by a little-known figure named Ho Chi
Minh. In 1944 the American OSS parachuted in
U.S. military advisors and weapons to assist Ho in
his resistance against the Japanese occupation
forces which had overrun the French colony.
Despite the eventual defeat of Japan and allied
triumph in 1945, Roosevelt's higher vision would
die with him. History would take a more tortured
and bloody course in Vietnam.

The French colonial administration ruled pri-
marily through a "mandarin" system, which meant
that a small cadre of locals would act as agents for
the French. Most Vietnamese rightly saw these
agents as puppets for the French. These mandarins
were perceived as having sold out their country and
their own dignity to the French invaders. At the
same time, a tiny minority of French plantation
owners and local landlords confiscated much of the
farmable land. In essence, most of the land-owning
peasant population were enslaved in a serf-like
existence, working on plantations or doomed to
impoverishment as poor tenant farmers at the

mercy of ruthless landlords. Some of Nguyen Thi Dinh's most bitter memories were of the cruel village landlord barging into her home demanding unreasonable payments. She witnessed the shame of her parents' humiliating efforts to entertain and grovel before the landlord in desperate attempts to stave off collection. As a young girl she experienced the inequities of life, and she grew to hate the abuse of power by the French and their mandarin puppets.

The French colonial yoke represented not only an economic pillaging of coal, rice, tin and rubber, but a clash of civilizations. By 1910 the French had 45,000 bureaucrats living comfortably in the country. Only a handful bothered to learn the Vietnamese language fluently. The traditional Vietnamese educational system was dismantled and replaced by a French model, which stressed a French-only curriculum that was both alien and offensive to most Vietnamese. The new French system also offered far fewer opportunities for native Vietnamese, as there was a drastic shortage of French-trained teachers. The French colonial legacy was a Vietnamese population less literate than their forefathers had been. Vietnamese history, folklore and authors were marginalized and even deemed subversive. The spiritual encroachment of French Catholic missions was also disturbing to most Vietnamese, who viewed Christianity as a radical break from their own eastern religious traditions and culture. In short, the Vietnam of

Nguyen Thi Dinh's youth was one of economic drudgery seething with resentment.

But Nguyen Thi Dinh was very fortunate in one aspect. Since the nearest school was ten miles away, attending it was out of the question. Instead, Dinh was home-schooled by her older brother, Ba Chan, whom she adored. He taught her to love the native Vietnamese novelist Nguyen Dinh Chien, whose literary work stressed virtues of piety, loyalty, integrity, and good triumphing over evil. This was a timely and much remembered message for Dinh in a society inundated with stress and resentment.

By 1930, at the age of ten, Dinh noticed that Ba Chan "came and went at odd hours" and hosted clandestine meetings with other men. At one meeting Ba Chan handed her father a strange red cloth with embroidery on it. Though the curious little girl didn't know it at the time, she was witnessing the birth of a revolution. Days later that strange red cloth was hoisted and displayed as a hammer and sickle flag at a prominent river junction near her town. Soon after her beloved older brother Ba Chan was arrested as a subversive. Her grieving family was thrown into turmoil. It fell upon her to row a sampan two and a half miles every day to deliver food to her imprisoned brother. There she witnessed firsthand unspeakable brutality. Canton Chief Moun, also her parent's same tyrannical landlord, administered brutal beatings upon her brother and other prisoners. This went on for a year and a half until Ba Chan was released.

Upon his release Ba Chan explained to Dinh the difference between a subversive and a revolutionary. He told her that he was dedicated to the cause of making revolution "to overthrow the landlords who are oppressing and exploiting us, like Canton Chief Moun, and also the French who have stolen our country from us." Aside from the love and respect she held for her brother, even this simple twelve-year old girl could grasp the righteous anger and truth of her brother's words.

By her own admission, "I did not understand anything more than that the communists loved the poor and opposed the officials in our village." From age twelve, she ached to be a revolutionary but did not know how to become one. Her gender and place in society were as much an obstacle to her as the oppressive French. As a frustrated young girl, she mused, "It must be very difficult to make revolution, since I'm a girl I doubt if I can do that."

Over the next four years she increasingly would be torn between the paths of a committed revolutionary and the traditional societal expectations of marriage, family, and motherhood. By age sixteen this inner conflict came to a head. She clashed with her parents, who desperately wanted her to marry and settle down. They cajoled her with comments like, "State affairs are not for girls to take care of."

That she had blossomed into an attractive young woman who caught the eyes of many young men in her village further complicated matters. Several suitors sent matchmakers to her home with offers of marriage. Her parents, growing more desperate, pressed for her to accept.

Increasingly frustrated at their daughter's intransigence, Dinh's parents shifted their tactics. They tried to convince her that she was not up to the life of a revolutionary in terms of physical and moral courage or competence. She endured such barbs as, "And even if women can do it, they must be very capable. What can our daughter Dinh do? If she's caught, she'll confess everything and harm the others."

The more her parents pushed the more Dinh gravitated to an active role in the growing revolution. Unbeknownst to her parents, Dinh was already heavily involved in revolutionary activities in her village. By age sixteen she was handing out leaflets as well as performing courier and guard duties. She also spent time propagandizing local peasants, encouraging them to buy the local party newspaper.

Not surprisingly her parent's arguments fell on deaf ears and for good reason. Their arguments, which centered on her supposed ignorance, fearful consequences, and incompetence, only insulted the young Dinh. She was already fully aware of the consequences of failure or incompetence as a revolutionary. She had seen it firsthand while visiting her imprisoned brother. She had also confided early on to Ba Chan her desire to work for the revolution and postpone marriage.

For peasants like Dinh, the French colony of Vietnam, ruled through a mandarin system, resembled a polyglot of feudal kingdoms. Local canton chiefs wielded unchecked unilateral power in ruling their provinces, as if these provinces were their own personal fiefdoms. Vietnam was a land of fundamental inequities and a strong undercurrent of seething resentment. However, for the generation of Dinh and Ba Cahn there was a budding nationalism and an emerging awareness of communist ideology, which promoted the redistribution of wealth and the empowerment of working people. These two forces were very attractive to peasants, the majority of Vietnamese, for whom capitalism and democracy were synonymous with imperialistic exploitation. Dinh and her companions were ingrained with the conviction that they were seeking justice and were on the right side of history. The sympathy and support of the local population only reinforced those beliefs.

Mao Tse Tung stated that the successful revolutionary guerilla fighter is a "Fish that swims in the sea." Success means sustenance from the "sea," the sea being the indigenous population who provide food, shelter, weapons, and intelligence. Most peasants by definition live on the economic fringe, usually one bad crop away from ruin or starvation. They are conservative by nature and predominantly interested in the success or failure of their crops. For peasants to support guerrilla groups means a huge risk and sacrifice. Thus, for any revolutionary to be successful, his or her grievances, cause, and recommendations must be perceived as legitimate among the people. If a guerrilla group is able to operate, it is usually a very strong indicator that many people within the local population at least sympathize with their cause. Even more, it is certain that an undisclosed minority of people are actively aiding the guerillas.

The obvious solution to quelling an emerging revolution would seem to be for the sovereign authority to address the glaring social, economic, or political problems that are the root cause of dissent. Unfortunately, most emerging revolutions are usually met with even more repression, mostly in the form of military counter-insurgency operations. It is hoped that in this way the rebellion will be crushed in its infancy. This was the strategy of colonial French administrators and later the Americans. Not surprisingly, this repressive and violent approach only engenders greater resentment, which in turn creates a growing cycle of violence that usually provides greater support for the insurgent.

In 1938, Dinh thought she had found happiness. Her older brother had introduced her to Bich, a revolutionary colleague. Dinh and Bich shared the same goals of working for the revolution and immediately fell in love and married after a whirlwind romance. During that time both actively continued to work for the revolution. Dinh continued to work in the "Mutual Aid Association" and "Rice Transplanting Teams for Women." Both organizations were designed to assist peasants, but also raise their political awareness. Less than a year later, Dinh gave birth to their son, On. They could not have been happier. But it would be a short-lived happiness.

Three days after On was born, the security police barged into their home and arrested Bich. Dinh collapsed in grief. In July 1940 she was finally allowed to visit her husband. He then informed her that he had been given a five-year sentence to be followed by five more years of deportation. To make matters worse, when she returned home, she was arrested and detained for three weeks, during which she was interrogated about Bich and his associates.

At the end of her interrogation, she was informed that she too was to be imprisoned and was forced to give her seven-month old son to her mother. Again, she collapsed in grief. For days she couldn't eat and was almost catatonic. Just when she thought life could not get any worse, soldiers burst into her local prison, handcuffed her and another female prisoner, and threw them into the back of a truck. For two days they rode to internal exile at the infamous Ba Ra prison on the Cambodian border.

Ba Ra prison was southeast Asia's equivalent to

Devil's Island. Known for its "insalubrious" environment, it was located in a remote region infested with bugs, leeches, rats, and according to Dinh, "human beasts." It was the kind of place that "those who were sent there never came back alive." Upon arrival prisoners were greeted by Frenchmen with rattan whips who used these weapons for regular beatings. For three years she and other female prisoners performed hard labor, and were beaten and sexually abused by the guards. Those that refused the advances were beaten even more severely.

Three things kept Dinh sane and alive. First were the images of Bich and her son she kept always in her mind. She constantly dreamed of a "second wedding" with Bich. Second was the camaraderie of her fellow prisoners, both male and female. Third was the motivation and resolve steeled within her to continue to work for the revolution if and when she ever got out of prison.

At the end of 1943, on account of a cardiac disorder, she was released from Ba Ra prison and returned to her home to remain under house arrest. Three months later she received the devastating news that her husband, Bich, had died in prison. For an entire month she was an emotional wreck, consumed with grief over the loss of her husband, and haunted by nightly nightmares of Ba Ra prison. Most painful for her was trying to explain the loss to On, now almost four. At this low point in her life she entertained notions of becoming a Buddhist nun, or even committing suicide. Eventually the motive of revenge and love for her son pulled her out of her despair. Unfortunately, during her imprisonment and subsequent personal crisis, she had lost contact with the revolution.

At the same time, the forces of social norms and traditions began to close in on her, a fact of life she loathed as much as she loathed the French. In her words, "The life of a young widow like me in the old society was full of difficulties." The still attractive and young twenty-three-year old widow was again besieged by unwanted advances from village officials and soldiers, men she despised. The village chief, "a miserable old goat," pressed Dinh to be his concubine. He even enlisted his own wife in the effort to convince Dinh. How pathetic and degrading to women, the prideful Dinh thought, that men could force their own wives to recruit concubines for their husbands. For the rest of the year she fended off such indignities and worked to reestablish contact with the communist revolutionaries, now called the Viet Minh. After enduring imprisonment as well as the indignities foisted upon women by traditional society, Dinh was now convinced that more needed to be changed in her country than attaining independence and redistributing wealth.

The Spirit of 1776 and the
Long Haired Soldiers

In 1944 she finally reestablished contact with the Viet Minh. For her this was as much a family reunion as a return to the cause she cherished. Several colleagues had known Bich in prison and lovingly commented on how Dinh's son resembled his father. They also encouraged her to continue Bich's work for the revolution. In this she needed no exhortation. Nevertheless she felt warmed in the glow of this comradeship and closer than ever to Bich. What a difference between these men and the leering "mandarins" who had hounded her the past year.

Vietnamese history began to accelerate in the 1940s. For the Viet Minh, the advent of World War II brought opportunity and possibilities never before envisioned. In 1940 Nazi Germany overran France. Though France continued to maintain her colonies through the new Vichy government, there was the definite belief among natives in the colonies that France was fatally wounded, her imperialistic days numbered. Emboldened by this, Ho Chi Minh and his trusted subordinate and military genius, Vo Nguyen Giap, organized the Viet Minh and began outright military resistance. Though modest at first, it was a significant start.

In 1941 Japan entered the war and quickly overran much of Southeast Asia, including Vietnam. Though Japanese imperialism was just as exploitive as the French, the Japanese conquest had a huge psychological impact, because it demonstrated that France (especially white men in general) could be beaten. This further emboldened the Viet Minh in its embryonic stage. Ironically, for the sake of convenience, the new Japanese conquerors continued to administer the colony through the still intact French colonial administration. This fact only caused even deeper resentment against the French, who had been defeated, but easily acquiesced to the Japanese in the role of mandarin themselves. In the eyes of emerging Vietnamese resistance leaders like Ho Chi Minh, the French were not only exploitive, but morally bankrupt as well. To add insult to injury, Japan later disarmed the French colonial administrators and ruled the country directly themselves.

For Ho Chi Minh's Viet Minh WWII was a huge opportunity. Japanese defeat could by default leave a huge power vacuum in the country. During World War II, Ho Chi Minh's communist Viet Minh became the only effective nationalistic resistance group fighting the Japanese in Vietnam. Consequently the American OSS supported Ho Chi Minh's insurgents. On one occasion, Ho's life was saved from an acute attack of malaria and dysentery by an OSS airdrop of desperately needed medical supplies of quinine and sulfa drugs. Interestingly, in conversation with American OSS officers, Ho revealed a deep respect for America's struggle for independence. He also admired Abraham Lincoln. He felt that it was logical and natural for America to support the Vietnamese drive for independence against the Japanese and French.

By 1945 Ho's Viet Minh grew to a nationwide organization including under its umbrella thousands of resistance and freedom fighters and dedicated communists like Dinh. In every province and town, the Viet Minh established cadres in clandestine committee and "cell" structures to agitate and plan an impending takeover in anticipation of Japanese defeat and withdrawal. Dinh was a key leader in her native Ben Tre province in preparing for the uprising which became known as the "August Revolution."

In 1945, a week after Japanese surrender, Ho and his Viet Minh controlled Hanoi and proclaimed their new country The Democratic Republic of Vietnam. Viet Minh groups across the country seized control in this political and military vacuum. Once Saigon was in Viet Minh control, Ho gave a rousing speech from the roof of Hanoi's largest building. He declared independence to a tumultuous crowd of tens of thousands. In his speech he quoted the opening phrases of the American Declaration of Independence of 1776.

But the joy of newly declared independence was short-lived. Despite initial American reluctance for a French return to Vietnam, a new American administration under President Harry Truman saw things differently. The post-World War II ideological and political context had changed. The threat of worldwide communism and an emerging Cold War now dominated the thinking of American policy makers. The U.S. needed to rebuild a strong Western Europe as a bulwark against the menacing encroachment of the communist Soviet Union. Yet Western Europe was in shambles after the war. French leader Charles deGaulle made it painfully clear that the price of French cooperation in rebuilding Europe was U.S. acquiescence to a French return to their colonies. Still smarting from a humiliating defeat and the shame of Vichy rule, France looked to the return to their colonies as a way to restore national prestige. The new Truman administration reasoned that in the larger game of shoring up Western Europe and superpower politics, the Vietnamese backwater was expendable.

In late 1945 two divisions of French Soldiers sailed on American transports to Vietnam in order to reestablish colonial rule. Any attempt the Viet Minh made to negotiate was arrogantly dismissed. The French units arrived in November and promptly went about reestablishing control through arrests and massacres. In the face of this, Viet Minh like Dinh faded back into the countryside and went underground to reconsolidate for a war against the French. Repeated Vietnamese warnings about their will to resist were rebuffed. By 1946, the re-galvanized and ever-growing Viet Minh came out fighting and the French Indochina War was under way.

After 1945, at age twenty-six, Dinh's career took off. During the August Revolution, in the Ben Tre province, she helped rally and lead thousands in demonstrations for the new regime. She even held a position of honor as the flag bearer. After the uprising she was assigned leadership roles in her province's various Viet Minh's women's organizations. At the end of 1945, she was elected by her province to be on the executive committee of the Women's Liberation Association (WLA).

One of the most interesting and successful aspects of the communist Viet Minh (and later Viet Cong) revolutionary movement was its inclusion of women. As early as 1938, Vo Nguyen Giap wrote an influential book, *The Peasant Question*, which would exert significant influence on Vietnamese communists for many years in their approach to social and agrarian reforms. The book was an in-depth analysis of the conditions of Vietnamese peasantry and agriculture. Giap called for the fundamental need to redistribute land and dismantle the landlord system. Giap also outlined a host of social problems in need of reform; most radical among them were his views on liberating women. He deplored what he termed the "low position" of women in Vietnamese society and attacked numerous traditions such as early marriage, polygamy, and concubines. These only served to oppress and keep women as the "water buffaloes" of Vietnamese society. Giap's enlightened views on women would be an important cornerstone in the Viet Minh philosophy of a "people's war," which would require the full participation of both men and women to be successful. For women like Dinh, this was very attractive.

Ironically Dinh, like Air Marshal Dowding, would face the difficult challenge of changing mind-sets. Without effective leadership, the best of visionary ideas will remain ideas unless someone is willing to cross the threshold of inertia and turn ideas into reality. For many women, even though the new revolutionary ideology offered much promise, actually giving up the old traditions and status quo was only an idea. It would be Dinh who provided the key elements of personal example and persuasive leadership that mobilized the woman's liberation movement within the context of the on-going communist revolution. In fact there is strong evidence to suggest that one of the most popular and successful aspects of the communist movement were its women's organizations, most specifically the WLA. This was of immense importance to the Viet Minh and later the Viet Cong. By 1965, while fighting against the Americans, the WLA claimed 1.2 million members who performed a host of functions. Vietnamese women by the thousands regularly fought side by side with men. They also served crucial logistical and support functions as well. Women were the key gatherers and disseminators of intelligence, especially at village markets. Women were more often used as demonstrators because enemy soldiers would be more reluctant to respond with force.

Even more revealing was the fact that the WLA applied the "20% rule" in recruitment. The WLA, for the purposes of quality control, only allowed 20% of all applicants to perform duty and be awarded full membership. This suggests that the female response to join the revolutionary people's war was overwhelming, because the other 80% of potential applicants numbered approximately 4.8 million women.

Men like Ho or Giap did not overlook the many ways that Vietnam was a matriarchal society, particularly in terms of female management from households to village markets. It was only natural to use this instinct to their advantage. For westerners accustomed to viewing warfare and the profession of arms as a male domain, the Vietnamese experience was completely alien. During the war against both the French and the Americans, Ho and Giap had the theory and doctrine of female inclusion, but they needed role models for implementation. Dinh would rise to fulfill that role. Her "pocket biography" as a revolutionary was remarkable.

In 1945 she was the honored flag bearer of the August Revolution uprising in the Ben Tre province. That same year she was also elected to the Viet Minh province committee for Ben Tre. In

1946, she had a personal meeting with Ho Chi Minh. In 1954 she led the Kien Hoa province rebellion in support of the decisive battle at Dien Bien Phu. In 1960, she led another uprising against South Vietnamese President Diem. In 1961 she was promoted to command of the headquarters of all the central delta provinces. This was crucial, in that she had made the jump from a local provincial leader to command of a regional unit. In 1964 she was appointed a member of the Presidium of the National Liberation Front (NLF), the overarching governing body of communist forces fighting against the Americans and the client state of South Vietnam. In 1965 she was made chairman of South Vietnam's WLA. Later that year, she was appointed Deputy Commander of the entire NLF, of which the WLA was a subordinate part. Her position as Deputy Commander was the equivalent to a two-star Major General's rank. She was technically the number two official in the chain of command, in charge of prosecuting the war on the ground. Her resumè as a revolutionary was as impressive as her wartime heroics. Women working for the Viet Minh became known as the Toc Dai, "long haired soldiers." For her prominent leadership among women's groups, Dinh eventually gained the national reputation as "Sister Ba of the long hairs." But this rise to prominence was not without tremendous sacrifice and commitment.

19 THE STRENGTH OF A WOMAN: DINH

IN HIS EPIC series about World War II, Winston Churchill titled one section The Locust Years. He used this phrase because even with the looming threat of a resurgent Germany, British defense budgets and resources remained sparse. This was immensely frustrating to British military leaders, who later barely survived the fury of German Blitzkrieg.

For Dinh the eight years between 1946 and 1954 were truly "locust years" of hardship, depravity and violence far beyond anything men like Winston Churchill and Hugh Dowding ever personally experienced. The French, anxious to restore control and national prestige, went about their task with a vengeance. The ranks of the French Foreign Legion eventually swelled to 350,000 men, many of whom were battle-scarred veterans of World War II and other colonial wars. Ironically, the commander of French forces, General Leclarc, prophetically stated that, "It would take 500,000 men to do it and even then it could not be done." Nevertheless, the French ruthlessly scoured the countryside, hunting down the Viet Minh and clearing areas of Viet Minh control.

In 1946, Dinh was given her first big assignment, an assignment that would carry her for the first time outside of her native Ben Tre province. She was to head a working delegation that was to travel to Hanoi and meet Ho Chi Minh. The purpose of the delegation was to coordinate with the central committee for actions in the south. In Hanoi Dinh met Ho and was inspired by his vision of independence and example of personal humility. Upon her return south she was placed in charge of smuggling by sea one thousand rifles and assorted ammunition back to her home province. For Dinh, who had never rowed anything larger than a sampan, to captain a large ship laden with weapons hundreds of miles through storms and French-patrolled waters was a harrowing experience. With gumption and a huge dose of physical courage she succeeded and was greeted as a hero back home. The delivery of one thousand weapons made a decisive difference for the Viet Minh in her area.

Viet Minh strategy, directed by Vo Nguyen Giap, was to present the French, and later the Americans,

with an unwinnable protracted "mosaic" war, a war
that would ultimately be won through the superior
will and commitment of the Viet Minh. To overcome the technical and firepower superiority of the
modern armies of France and America required the
extensive mobilization of the population, not just
men of draft age. Such a war was truly a "people's
war." The idea was twofold. First, tie down and frus-
trate the vast majority of the French forces, and later
the Americans, in chasing guerrillas. Second, deploy
newly raised conventional Viet Minh forces against
the thinly spread ranks of the French in selected engagements of Giap's own choosing. Though history
would record Giap's strategy as brilliantly successful,
for those engaged in the fighting at the local level it
was a tremendous sacrifice.

The entire countryside became a battle zone as
the fighting ebbed and flowed. In these years Viet
Minh guerrilla fighters like Dinh were constantly
on the run in the deadly game of ambush, using
dangerous hit and run tactics. The French responded with large-scale sweeps through areas of
known resistance. The frustration level of the
French rose as they struggled with the exceedingly
difficult task of cornering an elusive enemy operating in their own familiar terrain. Fighting was
frequent and fierce with no quarter given. At one
point while hiding in a bunker Dinh was briefly
captured and brutally beaten with rifle butts. After
her "interrogation" she was saved from being raped

and executed by a timely Viet Minh counterattack. In the ensuing confusion she managed to escape.

In the swampy Ben Tre province where Dinh operated, she and her fellow Viet Minh lived on the very edge of starvation and survival. Rarely did they have more than a handful of rice to eat as a daily meal. In an attempt to control or purge "the sea" in which the Viet Minh guerrillas operated, the French resorted to desperate measures to deny access to certain areas. It was common for the French to fill in or poison many wells. As Dinh recalled, they had to "shed blood to obtain drinking water."

In her memoirs, Dinh makes constant reference to working in the fields and rice paddies. A very important aspect of the communist philosophy was the personal examples set by communist leaders as they shared the burdens of the common peasant. This was not some hollow political gesture made by transparent politicians. For the Viet Minh cadre in her province, the policy was that each was to till a "cong" (small parcel) of land when and wherever possible. Dinh believed that for many years she spent up to fifty percent of her time working with farmers in the fields. Such a policy kept Viet Minh leaders like Dinh both humble and in touch with the very people they hoped to recruit and lead. This policy went a long way toward earning credibility for the communist leadership.

By 1954 the war had turned dramatically in favor of the communists. The French, tiring of war, searched for a decisive battle. They established an elite large force in the Dien Bien Phu Mountain valley, straddling key lines of communication and supply routes in northern Vietnam. Their plan was to goad the majority of Giap's forces into the open in a single battle where the French could slaughter the Viet Minh with superior firepower. The French plan assumed the Viet Minh lacked the heavy weapons, logistical and transportation means to sustain a large battle in the remote mountain valley. The French were wrong.

In eight years of fighting, the Viet Minh had captured more than enough heavy weapons and ammunition. In an amazing logistical feat, lacking the necessary automotive transport, the resourceful Viet Minh "Legion of Porters" disassembled the heavy ordnance and hauled it on their backs piece by piece, shell by shell to the battlefield. Giap then ringed the high ground surrounding the French garrison with artillery, and settled in for a long siege. Throughout the rest of the country, Giap simultaneously unleashed coordinated guerrilla attacks, effectively tying down French forces and preventing French large-scale counterattack or reinforcement.

In support of Giap's grand strategy, Dinh led the Kien Hoa province rebellion south of Saigon in early 1954. The efficiency and ferocity with which she pressed home her attacks was astounding. She not only succeeded in tying down enemy forces, but also succeeded in liberating vast areas, helping to trigger a collapse of French control in the strategically vital Mekong River area around Saigon. The French garrison at Dien Bien Phu was isolated and could only be resupplied by air. After months of bombardment, Giap's forces overran the garrison and won a stunning victory that shocked the world. For the first time in history a poor peasant army had defeated a modern western military power. This same strategy would also be used in 1967 and 1968 against the Americans at a place called Khe Sanh before and during the infamous Tet Offensive of 1968. Faced with disastrous reversals in both north and south, the French took to negotiations to end the conflict.

The Geneva Conference was formed to negotiate the French withdrawal, reaching an agreement known as the Geneva Accord in 1954. The country was to be temporarily divided at the seventeenth parallel for administrative purposes. Ho Chi Minh's Communists would control the northern half of Vietnam while the southern half would remain under French control. France was to eventually withdraw their colonial administration in the south as well and let the southerners seek their own national determinism. Of course the French hoped the south would remain part of the "French Union." A nationwide referendum was to be held in 1956 to unify the nation politically.

With the collapse of the French, America rushed

into the vacuum of Vietnam. America was determined not to let another country fall to communism and stemming the tide of communism dominated American policy. By now America had romanticized the French war in Vietnam as a kind of crusade against communism. In fact, by the 1950s, America was underwriting almost the entire cost of the French effort. Having been an observer at the Geneva Conference but not a signatory, America felt no obligation to uphold the accords.

American policymakers were in a quandary. It was a foregone conclusion that Ho Chi Minh would easily win the 1956 national elections because he was a national hero equivalent to a Vietnamese George Washington. Ho was one of the few national leaders who had not sold out to the west. He was the liberator from the dreaded French. To hold the elections would be to acquiesce to the entire country being politically unified under communist leadership. American policymakers viewed that conclusion as unacceptable. We were determined not to let another "domino fall."

American advisors, working feverishly to establish a working democracy in the southern half of the country below the seventeenth parallel, knew the overwhelming popularity of Ho Chi Minh. Fearing a communist victory at the ballot box, the U.S. canceled the nation-wide elections. America was now firmly committed to a nation-building project in South Vietnam. Ho Chi Minh and leaders like Dinh were furious at this American betrayal of the Geneva Accords and the Vietnamese people by not allowing them to vote for their own destiny. The Americans had negated years of fighting the French for independence. Ho had only won a half-victory in securing North Vietnam as a sovereign state. Ho's pleas to the west were ignored. Yet if Ho and his communists could not unite the country politically through elections they would do so through military force.

Unfortunately America's well-intentioned nation-building project in South Vietnam was plagued from the beginning by a host of problems that were never resolved. First and foremost, the Vietnamese leaders selected by the U.S. were either incompetent or rejected by their own people. Most Vietnamese saw the Americans as mere replacements of the French. South Vietnamese saw their newly appointed leaders as the new "mandarins" of the Americans. People like Dinh wondered where these men were when they had been fighting the French. In Dinh's own words, these men were "Living in America in those years and getting fat on good food." Worse, most of these installed leaders had ties to and "baggage" from the French colonial regime.

One such leader, President Diem, epitomized all the problems. A Catholic in a Buddhist country, he was as incompetent as he was arrogant. With no political base other than his own family, he surrounded himself with equally incompetent family members to whom he entrusted much government power. Diem's Brother ran the secret police and gained a national reputation for being more cruel and ruthless than the French. Diem's wife openly joked of barbecues, referring to the Buddhist monks who burned themselves alive in protesting Diem's regime. Her remark reflected a disdain and arrogance on the part of South Vietnam's new leadership that was translated into deep resentment by the people.

Dinh bitterly recalls in her memoirs a visit of President Diem's to villages in her area. Diem's entourage, dressed in western business suits and starched American fatigues, arrived in a caravan of black limousines, surrounded by dozens of security police. This image contrasted sharply with Ho Chi Minh, who walked freely among his people in sandals and modest native garb. The communist leadership, like Dinh, projected an image of humility and servant leadership. Leaders like Dinh not only projected these values, but also had the strength of character to live them out daily in front of the people.

Aside from being disconnected from their people, South Vietnamese leaders, more interested in self-aggrandizement and nepotism, consistently pursued disastrous domestic policies. After victory at Dien Bien Phu, the communist cadres in the south had run off the landlords and redistributed much of the land. This was very popular. However, as the embryonic South Vietnamese regime established itself, it reconfiscated land and reinstated many of the old landlords who often demanded exorbitant back rents. The peasantry was incensed. In an effort to wrest the rural population from communist control, the South Vietnamese government forcibly moved thousands of peasants off their land in the unsuccessful "Strategic Hamlet" and "Agroville" programs. Also, Diem's regime, in the attempt to round up communists, arrested many people who had fought with the Viet Minh for independence against the French. This was hugely unpopular. Dinh herself was again on the run when the new government placed a substantial bounty of 10,000 piastres on her life "to anyone who can apprehend Nguyen Thi Dinh, an extremely dangerous Viet Cong Female." The people generally viewed these measures as the new mandarins reasserting a new form of western imperialism. The American rhetoric concerning the benefits of democracy and capitalism were undermined by a miscarried reality on the ground.

By the 1960s approximately half the land in South Vietnam was owned by less than one percent of the population. This was a recipe for disaster. In Dinh's words, "the flames of hatred smoldered in the hearts of people." Ironically, repression and exploitation are not American values. The cancellation of national elections and the coercing of a population into hopeless tenant farming arrangements are not the economic model nor political ideal approved of by most Americans. The Viet

Minh in South Vietnam realized that the new regimes offered no hope of accommodation or reform. Consequently, the Viet Minh, reorganized and renamed the Viet Cong, began to fight back. In 1960, Dinh lead another uprising in her province against the Diem regime. In her own words there was "no other road to take" (this phrase became the title of her memoirs published in 1968). The second Indochina war was underway.

That America would eventually invest an army of over half a million men at the cost of over 50,000 killed in upholding such an unworkable and corrupted regime is a tragedy. In the name of fighting communism, America, in a very real sense, fought to uphold inequities not endorsed in our own country. Many of these inequities and contradictions were noticed and reported by American military personnel. In retrospect, it is a wonder that U.S. Army morale held up as long as it did and the problems like "fraggings" (deliberate attempts by subordinates to kill or wound their own officers) were not more prolific. All the applied firepower we would bring to bear could not reconcile the underlying contradictions and inequities that people like Dinh stood against. In fact the more firepower we brought to bear only generated more collateral damage and further resentment on the part of the Vietnamese people caught in the crossfire.

Not surprisingly, the Viet Cong made rapid gains against the fledgling and unpopular South

Vietnamese regime. Diem's leadership was so bad that even American advisors were relieved when he was deposed in a coup. This unfortunately led to a succession of revolving door leaders and coups within the South Vietnamese government. Even American President Johnson was disgusted with the turmoil and instability.

In trying to bolster the new regime, Americans began an ultimately unsuccessful strategic bombing campaign, "Rolling Thunder," to pressure communist leaders to surrender. It didn't work. In fact just the opposite happened. The more we bombed the more the conflict seemed to grow. By late 1964, Johnson's advisors gave him the chilling news that the Viet Cong were on the verge of complete takeover and only the introduction of American ground forces could rescue the situation. In March 1965 the Marines landed at DaNang and began the rapid buildup of over half a million men in South Vietnam. America had taken over a war we barely understood. Though the French could not win this war with 350,000 men, America was convinced that with 550,000 men and more modern technology they could secure victory.

Dinh had since remarried to Hai Tri, another member of the Viet Cong. It was only after French defeat that Dinh could spend valuable time with her son On. When her husband became ill, the family considered evacuating north with On so they could be out of harm's way in the new round of fighting. Again Dinh had heart-wrenching choices to make. In the end, unwilling to abandon a lifetime of commitment to freedom and independence for a better world for her nation and her precious son, she and her new husband elected to stay south and sent nine-year old On to relative safety for schooling in North Vietnam. She plunged back into her work and organized the 1960 uprising against Diem in her province and began to brace for the American challenge.

Giap's strategic direction in the new war was essentially unchanged from the way he had fought the French. But for Dinh and the Viet Cong cadres of the NLF, changes had to be made. Though the entry of America was essentially a repeat of the fight against the French, the pace and ferocity of the conflict were greatly accelerated. American advantages in air power, rapid mobility of helicopters, and awesome firepower raised the stakes and required tactical adjustments on the part of the communists. Guerrilla fighters were now instructed to "grab the enemy's belts" and fight as close to the Americans as possible. Close battle would tend to negate the superior tactical air power of the Americans. Additionally, as with the struggle against the French, strict codes of conduct were developed for the Viet Cong in governing their behavior towards the peasants. High on the list was the prohibition of rape. Having been victimized in her own past, Dinh inherently knew the value of such policies. Her values were in direct contrast with the abhorrent conduct of the enemy, especially within the South Vietnamese Army.

Dinh also had to learn to think differently. She was no longer a tactical leader at the local level. In 1965, she was a two-star General, required to think in a larger context. Though Giap in Hanoi provided strategic guidance, at the end of the radio link it was Dinh who had to direct much of the operations on the ground in the southern war zone. Because of increased American effectiveness, Viet Cong casualties rose. Dinh's greatest challenge became mobilization and recruitment in order to sustain the war effort. This was as much a political as military task but nonetheless vital for the survival of the Viet Cong.

Dinh traveled extensively throughout South Vietnam in order to raise morale as well as provide direction. This was done at great personal risk. Traveling mostly at night in order to avoid air strikes, she crisscrossed the country. She was constantly on the run, dodging air strikes and massive ground sweeps, similar to the French operations. Her efforts were crucial because victory in such a "people's war" would depend as much a state of mind and morale as on actual battlefield victories. In fact, on fighting the more powerful Americans, battlefield victories were rare. In a war of attrition and wills, merely surviving by "staying in the game" was the real challenge for the guerrilla forces and the population willing to sustain them. The inspiration

and energy Dinh provided in motivating the troops
and mobilizing the population became the crucial
component to communist victory.

Ho Chi Minh's national recognition of Dinh was
a testament to her importance. Additionally, the fact
that she held her position as Deputy commander for
ten years, from 1965 to 1975, was indicative of her
effectiveness. For ten years she provided stable
competent leadership under draconian conditions
as her fellow countrymen reeled under the unre-
lenting assault of American firepower. She was the
only woman in the world to hold such high rank and
crucial position for so long. She has no female coun-
terpart in modern western armies.

After the infamous Tet Offensive of 1968, at
which Dinh was instrumental in the mobilization
and conduct of the Viet Cong, America sought to
disengage from a now-recognized unwinnable conflict. Though the war would drag on for several
more years, America had lost its will to fight.
Shortly after Tet, President Johnson went on national television and shocked the nation by saying
he would not seek reelection, and would instead de-
vote his energy to the search for peace. The shock
waves of the Tet Offensive had broken not only
Johnson's presidency, but also America's will to
fight. Richard Nixon was elected president and subsequently implemented "Vietnamization." In
essence the Americans were to turn the brunt of the

war back over to the South Vietnamese government as the U.S. began a slow, phased withdrawal. What this really signaled was a long retreat.

Though Tet was a turning point, it was not without cost. The Viet Cong cadres that Dinh had built up for years were decimated in the nationwide assaults that ran smack into the maw of American firepower. Estimated Viet Cong casualties ran over 50,000. The butcher's bill was indeed high. As a result, after 1968, much of the war effort in the south was assumed by increasing numbers of Giap's North Vietnamese Army (NVA), regular soldiers making the hazardous journey to the south down the Ho Chi Minh Trail. Despite unflagging communist commitment to the war, the tremendous losses did affect morale in the Viet Cong camp. Just holding on until America completed withdrawal was a huge challenge for Dinh. After 1968, much of her efforts involved the coordination of the use of NVA regulars and the reconstitution of the Viet Cong. Quite simply, she was viewed as the stabilizing influence within the NLF during these tumultuous years. By 1975 America had fully withdrawn and Saigon fell. It was over.

After unification in 1975, Dinh was transferred to Hanoi and finally enjoyed a reunion with her son, continuing to pursue a career in the communist government. She eventually became president of the national Woman's Union and Vice-President of the Council of State, both high positions. Much of her efforts were now directed to rebuilding the ravaged country.

"The Strength of the Whole Forest"

Communist victory in Vietnam over two western military powers was nothing short of remarkable. Reams of materials have been written on Vietnam. Most of what has been written focuses on the dissection and analysis of failed policies, lack of unified strategy or clear objectives on the part of U.S. military and political leaders. But the life and career of Senior General Nguyen Thi Dinh gives us another more penetrating perspective on both the conflict and the subject of leadership.

A great lingering question about the American conflict in Vietnam haunts us today. How could America, with the best of intentions, not effectively rally the South Vietnamese people to the worthy causes of freedom and democracy? Even with the use of a huge army and billions of dollars in foreign aid, the U.S. could not seem to get the Vietnamese people to fight and die for our causes as well as communists like Dinh could for theirs. Some analysts point toward flawed policy and decision-making. Others point towards the rising tide of an attractive communist ideology, coinciding with the breakup of the colonial empires in Post World War II. But the question still remains. How did communists convince the poor farmer to throw down his plow and pick up an AK-47 assault rifle? The answer is not to be found in policies or ideologies. The answer is to be found in leadership, most specifically in the leadership of a woman like General Dinh.

The peasants of Vietnam were drawn into history's swirling vortex of the conflicting ideologies of communism, capitalism, democracy, colonialism, imperialism, nation building and the Cold War. After the French departure, the Vietnamese people were caught in the crossfire of competing visions for their country's future. One side, backed by the Americans, offered democracy and capitalism: the other offered communism. Both visions were worthy and noble ideals. In the struggle both sides, rightly or wrongly, pursued policies with the best of intentions. In the end, the people did not choose an ideology. They did not choose a policy. They chose leaders, specifically leaders like Nguyen Thi Dinh.

When circumstances of conflict, impoverishment and injustice closed in on the Vietnamese people, they did what all people do. They looked around for leaders who would help and guide them and evaluated those leaders carefully. What they saw of the mandarins, who served only the interests of the French and Americans, simply did not pass muster. The Vietnamese could fairly ask: Where were the South Vietnamese leaders like Diem during the struggle against the French? Who took my land? Who fought to get it back? Who bothered to work in the fields with me and get the crops in? Who taxes me the most? Who lives in decadence when I'm still poor? Who truly listens to my complaints? Who really cares about me? These are a host of fair questions and not one of them has anything to do with ideology. But they have everything to do with people and leadership.

In the final analysis, the communist victory in Vietnam, like the British in the Battle of Britain, was won on the basis of character. General Dinh's life stands as a testament to this. She did not have any of the formal military education of her French and American opponents. But she understood that the fundamental components of leadership were character issues more than mere competencies. Competencies can be developed through hard work, but character is forged over time. Dinh had the character to understand the notion of servant leadership and the guts to demonstrate it.

Dinh knew that the true function of a leader is to involve and serve those being led, not exploit them. She also knew that good leadership meant setting a personal example and sharing the burden of the people. This is easier said than done, but it is something people instinctively respond to. If Dinh was going to ask thousands to struggle for years, she knew she had to model sacrifice and commitment herself. It took the ingrained character traits of humility, perseverance, and hard work to spend countless hours and days on "rice transplanting teams," and tilling her "cong" of land with peasants. It also took the ingrained character traits of moral and physical courage to overcome obstacles, search for justice, and fight for the redress of lost dignity for herself, her society, and country.

Dinh herself said it best, "In struggling against the enemy, I had come to fully realize that we had to have the strength of the whole forest in order to be able to stay the force of the strong winds and storms." Like countless trees in a forest, bracing for a storm, the personal and professional struggle of Nguyen Thi Dinh hinged on mobilizing the only resource available, the forest of people. Other prominent communist leaders, like Ho and Giap, were brilliant in that they articulated correct strategy and inclusive social doctrine that provided a vision for victory. But it was Dinh, who in the toughest of times, breathed life into the fight in the southern half of the country. As a revolutionary leader of national prominence, she led by example and was vital in involving and mobilizing the other neglected half of society, women. She pioneered radical new visions of expectations for women and interdependencies between men and women, which were progressive and vital to success, both on and off the battlefield. By the thousands, women joined the struggle and helped tip the balance. If women were said to have been the "water buffaloes of Vietnamese society," then they surely became the "water buffaloes of the revolution," for without them the revolution could not have been won. Dinh's strength of character was the one element that could bind the numerous individuals of both genders into the strength of the forest. Dinh exhibited her character daily, in front of those she led, making their individual strength into a forest that could beat even a superpower.

20 IN THE END IT'S A QUESTION OF CHARACTER

IN 1531, Francisco Pizarro and a ridiculously small band of 180 men stood on the distant shores of modern day Ecuador. They had crossed an ocean from Spain to get there. They plunged inland and scant few years later they had conquered a continent. The world would never be the same. With literally a handful of men, Pizarro subjugated the Inca Empire numbering in the millions. Their conquest brought untold wealth to Europe and forever changed the lives of the people of South America through colonization and exploitation.

In the early 1980s a new breed of men, like their predecessors, stood on the shores of another vast yet unconquered continent, the continent of cyberspace. When they had conquered the uncharted territory our world was again transformed. When history books are written in the future, presidents or generals will not be as significantly remembered as men like Bill Gates. They "tuned us in" and put us "online." They, more than any politician, transformed our society and economy in the radical conversion to a "third wave" information age.

Like the original conquistadors, their task was immense, their beginnings humble, and their resources pitifully inadequate. Imagine that 180 men could discover and conquer a continent! And remember the critics of these new explorers — who would ever watch a 24-hour news station? Why would anyone ever need or want a personal computer in their home?

There have been other conquistadors. A rural monk, Martin Luther, and his 95 theses rocked a corrupt church and launched the Reformation. Four hundred years later a black minister bearing the same name, Martin Luther King Jr., boldly challenged the racial inequities of a country complacent in its prosperity.

No matter the realm, the common threads running through the lives of these conquistadors of past and present were their vision for the future and their commitment and love for their cause. Vision to see a goal no one else sees and the relentless heart to pursue it. Gustavus Adolphus, Napoleon, Dowding, and Nguyen Thi Dinh possessed these character traits. In the case of Napoleon, we observed that character, if not guarded, quickly reverts to costly excess and failure. Napoleon became a man no longer interested in serving France, but rather interested in using France as a personal instrument to further his own ambitions and glory.

We clearly see that a character out of balance will become self-destructive, forcing bad decisions, reflecting the internal selfishness and instability of the person making those decisions. What keeps the dreams from becoming nightmares? The selfless ingredients of our character work to keep our sinful tendencies in check. They are the internal qualities that harness our conquests for the betterment, not detriment, of man.

Ingrained core values much like Dowding's "Service and Manners," stressing selflessness, servant leadership, humility, and personal integrity are foundational. These are the "value behind the value." Interestingly and unavoidable is that these values are usually rooted in a person's deeply-held convictions or religious faith, which provide for them unassailable absolutes of right and wrong, good and evil. Temptations not consistent with the values ingrained in your heart are more easily recognized. They are indicators that your core values are being challenged. In a very real sense, you must build a "Great Character Wall" around yourself to guard your heart condition.

Genuine humility helps keep pride and ambition in check. Likewise, a servant's heart constrains self-destructive greed and selfishness. Well-placed trust and confidence enacted through involvement and interdependence go far in assuaging the destructive forces of fear, mistrust, and accepted mediocrity.

A genuine leader sees him or herself as an instrument to further the goals of the organization, as opposed to the organization existing for his own self-aggrandizement. The rules and structure of an organization are blended into a prosperous relationship, not a stifling regimen existing to reinforce a hierarchical status quo. By doing this, the door to action is opened, giving a leader the confidence and trust to involve and invest capable subordinates with more authority and power.

Against the longest of odds and worst of circumstances, leaders like Gustavus, Napoleon, Meade, Dowding, and Nguyen Thi Dinh were consistently able to rally people to their cause. Their character was a catalyst for empowerment. Though respectful of traditions and societal norms, they, especially Nguyen Thi Dinh, were not held captive by these traditions.

Not everyone reading this book is going to try and conquer continents or transform economies. The quest of man or woman does not have to be grand to be significant or of value. It can be the unheralded reconciliation of a separated couple in healing a broken marriage and mending a family. It can be the thankless and tireless community social work of a volunteer in a sea of urban blight, for this is as vital as are record profits and appearing on the Fortune 500 list.

In farming, when wheat and chaff are separated, both are tossed into the air. The wheat, having more useful substance, falls back into the pan to be preserved. The chaff, having much less substance, far more subject to the whims of even the mildest of air currents, is easily borne on the wind and aimlessly carried away. Like the wheat and the chaff, we will all be tossed into the rough and tumble of life.

In a sense we all desire to make a difference. To some degree or another, we all possess vision and heart. From battlefields to business, the sword will be wielded. In pursuit of our dreams, let us not so much depend on the "color of our money," but rather, in the words of Martin Luther King Jr., on the "content of your character." Our good character creates in us worthy substance, which like the wheat, falls back into the pan to be retained for beneficial use. Struggle always to be wheat rather than chaff.

BIBLIOGRAPHY

Aubry, Octave. *Napoleon*, (New York, 1964) p. 20

Bourrienne, Louis de. *Memoirs of Napoleon Bonaparte*, ed. by R.W. Phipps (4 vols,; New York 1885), I, p. 318.

Brengle, Samuel. *Salvation Army*, 1887.

Chandler, David G. *The Campaigns of Napoleon*, (New York, 1966) p. 291.

Ibid., p. 293.

Connelly, Owen. *Blundering to Glory*, Scholarly Resources INC. Wilmington, Delaware, 1987.

Dinh, Nguyen Thi. *No Other Road to Take, Memoirs of Mrs. Nguyen Thi Dinh*, Data Paper: Number 102, Southeast Asia Program, Department of Asian Studies, Cornell University, Ithaca, N.Y. 1976., p. 22.

Ibid, p. 24.

Ibid, p. 25.

Ibid, p. 27.

Ibid, p. 27.

Ibid, p. 27.

Ibid, p.27.

Ibid, p. 28.

Ibid, p. 33.

Ibid, p. 35.

Ibid, p. 44.

Ibid, p. 50.

Ibid, p. 51.

Ibid, p. 61.

Ibid, p. 77.

Donnithorne,Larry. *The West Point Way of Leadership*, Currency Doubleday, New York, 1993, p 164.

Ezekiel 22: 30

Giap, Vo Nguyen. *The Peasant Question, 1937-1938*, Cornell University Press, Ithaca N.Y., 1974. The book was first published by an underground press in Hanoi in 1938.

Griess, Thomas E. *The Dawn of Modern Warfare*, Avery Publishing Group Inc. Wayne, N.J., 1984., p.102.

_____. *The Wars of Napoleon*, Avery Publishing Group INC. Wayne, N.J. 1985., P. 26.

Ibid, p. 109.

Ibid, p. 127.

_____. *The Second World War, Europe and the Mediterranean*, Avery Publishing Group Inc. Wayne, N.J. 1984, p. 56.

Halberstam, David. *HO*, Alfred a. Knopf, New York, 1971, p. 116.

Luke 7:1-10

Manchester, William. *The Glory and the Dream*, Little, Brown and Company, Boston, 1973, p. 923.

Markham, Felix. *Napoleon*, (New York, 1963) p. 26.

Ibid, p. 188.

Morgenson, Gretchen. *The Captains Who Didn't Go Down with the Ship*, Forbes Magazine, August 21, 1989., p. 39-41.

Napoleon I, Correspondance de. (32 vols,; Paris 1858-1870) XI, No. 9393, p. 336.

Patton, George S. *The Cavalry Journal*, September 1933.

Shakespeare, William. *Anthony and Cleopatra*, act iii, sc. I, L. 22.

Tung, Mao Tse. *On Guerrilla Warfare*, The Nautical and Aviation Publishing Co. of America, Baltimore, Maryland. 1992., p.113.

Ibid, p. 100-102.

Tuchman, Barbara. *The March of Folly*, Ballantine Books, New York, 1984., p. 244.

Ward, Geoffrey C. *The Civil War*, Alfred A. Knopf Inc. New York, 1990., p. 256.

Wright, Robert. *The Man Who Won the Battle of Britain*, Charles Scribner's Sons, New York, 1969, p. 23.

Ibid, p. 26.

Ibid, p.17.

Ibid, p. 280.

Ibid, p. 280.

Ibid, p. 283.

ABOUT THE AUTHORS

LCDR. THAD A. GAEBELEIN, USMM, is a former Army major who has taught military history at West Point. He has also served as an Infantry officer and an assault helicopter pilot. He has served as headmaster of a prestigious private school and is currently an Instructor at the U.S. Merchant Marine Academy in Kings Point, NY.

RON P. SIMMONS is the Chief Operating Officer (COO) of Viatech, Inc., a multi-million dollar Information Packaging Company, and the author of the highly praised text *Value-Directed Management: Customers, Organizations and Quality*. Additionally, he has written numerous publications on "the creation of value" and interdependence within organizations.

Though Ron currently resides with his wife and three children on the North Shore of Long Island N.Y., he has traveled extensively around the world sounding the "battle cry" of values.